A ROYAL RECLUSE

Memories of Ludwig II. of Bavaria

by

Werner Bertram

Translated
by Margaret McDonough

With coloured frontispiece,
20 coloured and 16 black-and-white plates

1st - 4th thousand

Published by Martin Herpich & Son, Engravers and Publishers
Munich 54, Abensberger Straße 4

To commemorate the 50th anniversary of the death of the ill-fated King: 13th June 1936. Written in deepest reverence and devotion.

THE AUTHOR.

Chief persons:

Ludwig II., King of Bavaria.

Prince Otto, the King's brother.

Marie of Bavaria, the Queen-Mother.

Hofrat von Pfistermeister, secretary to the Cabinet.

Richard Wagner, poet-composer, conductor of the royal orchestra.

Princess Sophie.

Elisabeth, Empress of Austria.

Maria Alexandrowna, Empress of Russia.

Prime Minister von Lutz.

Prince Chlodwig zu Hohenlohe.

Prince-Regent Luitpold von Bayern.

Count von Holnstein.

Karl Theodor, Baron von Washington.

Obermedizinalrat Dr. von Gudden, director of a lunatic asylum.

Dr. Müller, assistant-doctor.

Count Alfred von Dürckheim, personal aide-de-camp.

Karl Hesselschwerdt, Quartermaster at Court.

Mayr, the King's personal valet.

Weber, valet in Neuschwanstein.

Osterholzer, the King's personal coachman in Hohenschwangau.

•

All places and dates are strictly historical.

Scenes,
in the order of their succession:

I. The young King.

Munich, the 25th August 1845!

Thunder of cannons . . .

Within Castle Nymphenburg, the Crown Princess Marie of Bavaria had waited twelve long hours for the birth of the future King. The new-born babe, upon whom a great and illustrious future smiles, is named Ludwig, after his grandfather.———

Bavaria, which through Napoleon I. had become a kingdom and which also through the medium of Napoleon, as well as later by the provisions of the Congress of Vienna in 1815 was considerably increased in size, now took its place at the head of the smaller German States. Ludwig I., who erected the wonderful "Walhalla" near Regensburg, had, by consistently patronising the Arts during his reign, transformed Munich, formerly nicknamed the "Beer Town", into a cultural centre.

The events of 1848, ending in the forced abdication of the first Bavarian king, placed his son Maximilian on the throne. He, although a follower of the then fashionable liberalism and surrounding himself with free-thinking counsellors, withstood the foundation of a German Empire under Prussian leadership and refused to acknowledge the Imperial Constitution.

As his father before him had thought to benefit his land by furthering the Arts, so the son by advancing the cause of Science hoped to raise the general standard of culture in the country. He therefore called to the University of Munich, scholars of outstanding repute and founded what was called the Historical Commission.

The favourite sojourn of Maximilian was, until the day of his death, the castle at Hohenschwangau. Not only did he rebuild it, but had it richly decorated by famous artists. And here it was that the grandson of Ludwig I. was destined to pass a sunny, carefree childhood.

*

Hohenschwangau!

What a splendid German name ! (See plate 2.)

High over the forest stands the old lake-castle like a fairy fortress of far-forgotten days. From the hill whereon it has stood these many hundreds of years, its ochre-yellow bastions stand out in striking contrast to the green forest. Here sang the Minnesinger Hiltebold of Schwangau. Here, sad and heavy-hearted, the mother of Konradin of Hohenstaufen bade farewell to her son when he started on his fateful journey into Italy. And here also the Emperor Ludwig the Bavarian, and the Emperor Maximilian I., found needful rest.

> This home of ancient lineage
> Looks far o'er alpine land.
> Here strings of throbbing love-lute

Bild 2: Schloß Hohenschwangau
Hohenschwangau Castle

Bild 3: Bildnis des Kronprinzen Ludwig

Nach einem Aquarell von E. Rietschel von 1850   Portrait of the Crown Prince Ludwig
König Ludwig II. Museum in Herrenchiemsee

S. M. König Max II. v. Bayern
mit Gemahlin und Kronprinz Ludwig.

Bild 4

Were plucked by royal hand.
And still through moon-swept valleys
The Minnesinger's song
Thrills o'er the hills to Untersberg,
Where Stauff has lain so long.
The limit of three countries,
Upon the wooded steeps,
The castle, like a sentinel,
Its guard of honour keeps:
And where Guelf, Stauff and Schyr
First drew their infant breath,
Flings now the tendrilled ivy
Its clinging cloak of death.

So sang Eduard Duller. And in the same spirit Maximilian II. created anew all the magic of the middle ages. For within the rooms, the walls are rich with colourful scenes: here reigns the world of long-ago. Brought to life by the magic of the artist's brush, the Swan-knight Lohengrin and Dietrich of Bern, side by side with Charles the Great and his courtiers, seem to breathe once more in life-like, realistic frescoes.

After their marriage Maximilian II. brought his young bride the Princess Marie of Prussia to this castle and in these frescoes, as in a picture-book, the little Crown Prince Ludwig read things that were destined to influence his whole mentality and to play a part in the tragedy of his life.

As wonderful as the castle itself, is the surrounding country. It would almost seem as if here perfection is reached. In sombre beauty the forest spreads its mantle over the hills: from out the bronze-green of the trees, two lakes,—the Alpsee and the Schwansee—shine crystal-clear, whilst high mountains fling protective arms around the silent spot.

In such perfect surroundings the beautiful Crown Prince and his brother Otto, grew up. Ludwig played very little with soldiers as did other princes and companions, but amused himself almost exclusively with a puppet-theatre and with curious figures and dolls. Even as a child he showed his repugnance for all that savoured of reality, living in a make-believe world of his own. As a boy he struggled fiercely against the cramming system of the school-room: with his passion for dreaming he conjured up scenes and shadows of his own imagining, lending them reality and finding therein his entertainment.

He never tired of listening, in childish ecstasy, to the wise, quiet voice of his mother relating:

"From the foam of a wave, Venus was born. The other waves, jealous, complained to Father Zeus of this favouritism, at which Zeus, the Almighty, stretching out his hand, took foam from the jealous waves, creating therefrom . . the Swan! Upon the water the swan now moves majestically, the waves carrying him proudly. Wise is his eye and snow-white his pinions, but should the hunter's bullet find him, his death is a slow fading to sweet music."

This and other such tales made a great impression on the young Prince and all his life he retained a special affection—for swans.

Years passed.

The two Princes passed from childhood to youth. Their father Maximilian inflicted a spartan education on his sons, allowing of no effeminate influences. In consequence, the young Crown Prince was seldom allowed to come down to the palace in Munich remaining for the most part under the spell of the fantastic world he had created for himself.

Was it surprising therefore, when Ludwig grew up that he showed signs of unsociability, was recluse and found no points of common interest with his stern father? Even on the day of his coming of age, the only real interest he showed was in the illuminating of the old castle.

In spite of this lack of understanding between father and son, it was the example of his father's simple sense of citizenship which paved the Crown Prince's way later on to the hearts of his people. The adoration of this alpine people for their handsome Prince first took root in the hill-village, to spread later over the whole of Bavaria. And wherever the Crown Prince went he reciprocated this simple devotion, devoid of all false pride, taking interest in the smallest details, even making many little personal sacrifices on behalf of his people.

To the old and sick he sent his own doctor with medicines and delicacies. For many a young couple he provided the dowry and climbers who had lost their way he rescued, often at great personal danger. On Midsummer-Day he took part in the festivities, dancing with the villagers under the village lime tree, jumping through the fire as is the old custom, singing and yodelling after the manner of all alpine dwellers.

Contrasting strangely however, came days when the Prince, who was of a somewhat melancholy disposition, would sit hour after hour alone in the bay-window thinking, or at the little piano, picking out strange chords: days when, bareheaded, he would ride out from the glimmering castle by moonlight to the nearest forest-clearing, where, dismounting, he would lead his horse mile after mile, tramping beside it through the solitary night.

And on many a summer night a boat slid over the Schwansee, idyllic, · on moonlit waves, wherein was a slender, ardent youth, reciting as he rowed, favourite stanzas from Schiller'spoem: "*Seid umschlungen, Millionen ——diesen Kuß der ganzen Welt!*" ("With this kiss let me embrace, the many millions of the world!") His voice vibrates over the listening lake, whilst the moon-burnished wavelets ripple an accompaniment.

*

1864.

Again the spring heralded its approach in the alpine valley of "Schwanengau". Gone was the snow, once more the great forests and the rock-faces of the mountains were reunited. Quiet at last, after the storms of winter, the blue surface of the lake reflects trembling pictures, and only in the far distance, on the frontiers of Tyrol, do the highest peaks show gleams of snow.

Through the little village of Hohenschwangau two carriages were coming from the direction of Füssen, bringing a deputation from Munich. They turn out of the high-road to the right, making towards the old castle of the Wittelsbach family. In the tree-shadowed castle court five gentlemen get out, climb slowly and thoughtfully the old stone steps, waiting beneath the Gothic entrance for admittance.

In vain the adjutant seeks the Crown Prince, rushing from room to room of the castle,——Ludwig is nowhere to be found, for he is reading, half-hidden, down by the splashing fountain, oblivious to hurrying footsteps, absorbed in the text of Richard Wagner's *Lohengrin*.

At last they have found him. Breathless his adjutant stands before him:

"Your Royal Highness——a Deputation from the Ministry on urgent state-affairs, requests audience."

"Show the gentlemen out here then."

"Excuse me, your Royal Highness, but they are a Deputation from His Majesty the King——"

"Well, what of that? Can't the gentlemen manage to come as far as this?"

"If your Royal Highness commands——"

But Ludwig sprang up suddenly, pacing restlessly to and fro. Had he a premonition of what was coming? As he watched the gentlemen of the Deputation approaching, he was struck by their earnest mien.

"Your Royal Highness! On behalf of her Majesty the Queen and in the name of the Government, we beg your immediate presence in Munich. The health of His Majesty the King is in danger, the doctors expect the worst."

The chill of sudden silence fell upon the little group after these solemn words. The Crown Prince had suddenly sprung up. A head taller than them all, he stood before them now, in all the wonder of his youth, clad in a light blue velvet cloak, up-standing as a fir-tree, as beautiful as a young Apollo, in the spring sunlight. His thoughts still caught in the meshes of the poetry he had been reading, he wrestled with reality.

After a moment he answered like an obedient son, with three words:

"I will come."

The Deputation withdrew, bowing.

The death-knell of his carefree youth had sounded.

*

On the 10th March of the year 1864, Maximilian II. of Bavaria died. Towards the end, father and son talked long together alone. The King made a last effort to win the confidence of his son who had always avoided contact with his father and whose character remained for him a closed book. No one will ever know what passed between them, nor whether at the eleventh hour the gulf between them was bridged over. The King's farewell to his family was simple and touching, but his last words were reserved for his successor:

"My son, I hope that for you Death will come as quietly as he has come for your father!"

The deeper significance of these words remains a tragic mystery. Was the veil of the future lifted that the dying eyes might pierce beyond? On the threshold of Death was it given to the dying man to see the tragic end which awaited his son?

Overwhelmed with an almost childlike grief Ludwig left the death-chamber——but already the first page bowed low before him with the fateful words:

"Your Majesty!"

The young man started back, visibly shocked. What a weight of responsibility lay in that one word: Majesty! So much power was his, from now onwards. He could now do what he wished and how he wished, none could stand in his way. With him rested decisions which could fling the country into war and destruction, or raise it to the highest levels of culture and prosperity. Nothing remained closed to him: at eighteen years old, the world lay before him.

Beyond the Palace gates knelt a crowd of many thousands, some sobbing, all praying. Will this all too early call to king-ship to one so young, bring blessing on the land and crown, or does this sudden death portend sorrow for the future? That none could prophesy what lay in wait, was providential.

Ceremony followed ceremony. The troops took the oath of allegiance to the new King. Maximilian died in the early morning. In the afternoon of the same day, a Herald in traditional uniform accompanied by two drummers, rode through the town, proclaiming amidst the roll of muffled drums, the accession to the throne of Ludwig II. of Bavaria. And the next day Ludwig himself took the oath of Constitution.

"The King is dead——long live King Ludwig!" The uninterrupted cheers of the people were nerve-racking to the youth of barely nineteen. They gave him an ovation, one after the other came to do homage to him and still the cheering rose and fell outside the Palace.

Then came the day when the newly crowned King with his brother Otto, followed the coffin of their father through the streets of Munich, dignified in personal sorrow. He walked as a Prince in the olden times, simply, unaffectedly, a veritable Fairy Prince he seemed.

His unusual height accentuated in comparison with others, he slowly passed by the grave of his father, treading a solitary path towards a tragic destiny.

*

"It has pleased Almighty God to call my beloved father away. There are no words which express my feelings. Hard and heavy with responsibility are the tasks before me, but I trust in God that He will send light upon my way and power to fulfil my duties. I will govern in accordance with my oath and with the constitution, which has been maintained for half a century. The prosperity of my beloved Bavaria and the upholding of Germany's greatness shall be my aim and I beg you all to stand by me and to assist me to fulfil these my duties."

This was the text of the young monarch's speech in answer to the Prime Minister's address. It was an honest answer, free from empty phrases. To be king meant, for Ludwig II., from the first day of his reign, to be nothing less than God's representative in all worldly matters, to strive only for the highest ideals, both in his private life and for his people.

His ideal was a kingdom where peace, joy, prosperity, contentment and general well-being for all should reign. That it should be granted him to rule over a land swayed by such ideals to the benefit and blessing of all, was his heart's desire.

Certainly, at the age of eighteen to be torn from the stillness of an alpine resort, plunged into the Court-life in Munich and so soon after to be called to the throne of Bavaria,—by nature somewhat imperious and obstinate as he was—seemed at the time to spell disaster. But in spite of prophecy to the contrary, everything went well. There was no change in the political or economical attitude of the government, Prime Minister von Schrenk remaining in office at first. Not until a year or so later was he succeeded by von der Pfordten. Ludwig II. had no greater ambition than to carry on the work of his grandfather and his father before him, to its natural conclusion. The chance of birth had set him at the head of the Bavarian people; God's will had made of him a king. History and tradition willed it so. Oblivion has claimed many kings and emperors, others achieved fame by war, very few shine by reason of great character and some have gone blood-stained to their long rest.

In governing his people, the young monarch set himself a special task. From the world-history of the past he would evolve a practical policy for the present: would forge the best weapons for the defence of throne and crown, harness the best plough to furrow the land and lastly he sought the best way to the hearts of his people. Patriotism and a foundation of splendid tradition, handed down from earliest times, was the heritage of the Bavarians. Now the call should go out to the greatest in the land to carry this great heritage forward and up to the highest pinnacles of achievement, in art and in politics.

A foundation had, however, first to be laid, for a people that delights in beauty must be shown beauty, must be taught to feel and to desire only the beautiful. Therefore a king who will govern by beauty must surround himself with perfection.

Ludwig II. himself, was a sovereign born to pomp and ceremony. From the day of his accession, no wish of his, however extravagant, failed to be realized. He appeared on the streets of the city, drawn by a golden coach, on special occasions donning his marshal's uniform, it's sky-blue cloth lending him a certain luminosity. Indeed, the King, with the white-bluish swan-feathers of his field-marshal's cap, completed a picture of striking beauty.

In every conceivable way the people gave expression to their loyalty and devotion for their young king. Always as he passed to and fro to Vespers the streets were lined with cheering crowds, and many a time, in the theatre, opera-glasses were directed away from the stage, to scan the finely-chiselled features of the young music-lover, whose dark eyes held that far-off look of the dreamer. Soon it became general knowledge that this personal beauty was only surpassed by his kindliness. In keeping with the whole magnificent build of the man were his fine eyes, in whose striking glance lay something visionary, almost unearthly. (See frontispiece.)

In private life, Ludwig II., in spite of all disappointments, remained strong in the faith of his Church. A small Russian triptych was his inseparable companion. This little Russian altar, of the finest Byzantine inlay, consisting of three separate parts, a present from the Empress of Russia to his father, went everywhere with him. When he moved to Munich, the Russian triptych went too, for at prayer before the beloved Image, his thoughts were carried back in loving gratitude to the happy years of his youth passed in Hohenschwangau. On his knees the young King breathed again the peaceful atmosphere of the silent old castle and there rose before his mind's eye the limestone crags where, in the wildest, most dangerous and inaccessible spot, it had ever been his wish to set a castle; or again he would feel the saddle of the beloved pony of his boyhood beneath him and wander once more in spirit through the wild valleys where the fragrant grass, starred with gentian, sloped down to two sapphire-blue lakes, reflecting high crags tufted with Alpine Rose and Edelweiss. All this beauty was irrevocably lost to him!

Speaking of this loss, Ludwig II. had once said: "Here I sit surrounded by heavy tomes and parchments, but I am not studying poetry as most people think, but International History and Statesmanship. It has been my fate to be called too young to face heavy responsibilities, too heavy for young shoulders, too difficult for a young brain, full till now of quite other thoughts and desires."

What was there about this royal youth, with his regal beauty, mated with melancholy? It was his inalienable right to become one of the greatest rulers in Europe. Why, even in his own capital must he fight and suffer, must he be doomed to disappointment, worry, betrayal and misunderstanding? What fate hung over him that at last he should be even driven into seeking seclusion?

It was his tragic destiny that all the inherited talents of this scion of the ancient House of Wittelsbach should grow to be an undeserved curse for himself but for the people of Germany a lasting blessing.

II. The Rescue of Richard Wagner.

Hardly fourteen days had passed since the death of King Maximilian.

Through the empty streets on Good Friday, a man was to be seen aimlessly wandering. Musician and revolutionary, without hope or plans for the future, he sought help in vain, in the face of a blustering March wind. Forced to fly from Vienna, he found shelter for a while incognito with old friends, until he should find some new means of subsistence. Flight had been forced upon him to escape many years of imprisonment as a debtor. Had one of his many creditors recognized him he would have been arrested on the spot on the score of his extravagance, his ruined married-life, his revolutionary ideas and his megalomania.

This man who had taken a room in the hotel "Bayerischer Hof" in Munich under an assumed name was not only in difficulties, but was on the verge of desperation, as he himself wrote at this time to a friend in St. Petersburg. Yet this man without position or posessions, destitute and ruined, was none other than Germany's greatest composer: Richard Wagner!

Even in Munich it was not long before Wagner once more began to feel the hand of those dreaded persecutors, his creditors. This eventually induced him to flee still further, this time to Zurich, where the wife of his friend

Wille, in the absence of her husband, took him into her hospitable house. Here, in the seclusion of the garden, the tormented man remained in hiding, occasionally taking long and lonely walks at the dead of night.

When his friend Wille returned, Wagner flew into a rage at their first interview, complaining that no one troubled about his great work, that his manuscript had been refused, and lay collecting dust on a shelf for lack of somebody with courage enough to take up the cudgels on his behalf. His nerves were on edge, his careworn face a mass of wrinkles and lines.

From Zurich he wrote to his friend Peter Cornelius, the famous painter:

"It is impossible for me to live so primitive a life as the organist Sebastian Bach. I simply *must* see light: some friend must arise who will help me, who will take my part. Then I shall be able to gather renewed strength and can repay his generosity——of that I am certain. But only a miracle can help me now, and that right soon, or I am done for!"

*

Four weeks after the accession of the new King, the following surprising conversation took place between the King and Hofrat von Pfistermeister, the secretary to the Cabinet:

"Has Your Majesty any particular wishes?"

"Well,——first of all I want to make Richard Wagner's acquaintance!"

"Really? But why, if I might put such a question?"

"If I remember rightly, it was about six years ago that my Father was persuaded by Duke Max, the great art-patron, to let *Lohengrin* be performed. Do you remember the occasion, Hofrat ?"

"I do indeed and it had a quite good reception too."

"Did my Father ever hear the opera again ?"

"Yes, four times, Your Majesty."

"Four times running ? Really ? Yet one could not maintain that he was very fond of opera, but that is not the point, Hofrat. What I remember so well is, as 15-year-old Prince hearing *Lohengrin*, with Ludwig Schnorr von Carolsfeld from the Dresden opera-house in the title role. At last I was considered old enough to be allowed to see it, after studying the legend of the Swan-Knight with my governess, Baroness Meilhaus. I was tremendously impressed by it. And do you remember what happened afterwards, Hofrat ?"

"Yes, one thing I remember was that after that time the ladies of the Court wore silver doves and swans in their hair and on their bodices."

"Yes, and then, the next day there was a reception in the Palace, and a little later on I found by chance one day a copy of Wagner's "The Art of the Future," lying on the piano at the house of Duke Max. Do you happen to know the book ?"

"No, Your Majesty."

"Then you don't know either Wagner's preface to his latest work called *Ring der Nibelungen* ?"

"Unfortunately not, Your Majesty."

"In the preface, this musician of the future—of the future, please notice—asks: 'Will a Prince ever arise who will enable me to produce my operas'."

At these words Pfistermeister started. Here then was the key to this remarkable conversation! Now it was his turn to answer and there was no getting out of it. Reluctantly he gave the cue for which the young King had been waiting, as he said: "Will *you* be that Prince? Does Your Majesty contemplate taking up this challenge?"

"That this as yet unknown man has a great mission to fulfil, is clear to me. In him I see a kindred spirit, indeed I may say that in him I see the object of my existence and I have an irrepressible desire to get to know him. You, Hofrat von Pfistermeister, will leave at once for Vienna, with an invitation to Wagner from me.—That's all, for the present. This is my particular wish, about which you enquired just now. You can prepare for your journey: here are my instructions to the Treasury ... thank you."

*

At a Committee Meeting of Munich Artists, Peter Cornelius, referring to the letter he had received from Wagner made the following remark, which was destined to become historical:

"Ludwig I. was keen on us painters; Maximilian on scholars and poets. How would it be, if for a change the present King were to be interested in music and were to take a fancy to Wagner?"

*

Hofrat von Pfistermeister had to return from Vienna without being able to carry out his mission: all he brought with him was a pen and a pencil of Wagner. Not even the composer's photograph could he lay before the King. Only considerably later did he discover the whereabouts of the musician, through the author Uhl, one of Wagner's friends.

Meanwhile, in the Palace, a King is waiting ...

While Pfistermeister continued his search, the unhappy composer himself arrived at Stuttgart to interview the conductor Eckert. One last desperate effort he made to get his *Tristan* accepted for performance, but in vain !

At this turning-point in his life, when Fame already beckoned to him, he was in the depths of the most acute mental depression, determined to renounce his art for ever. Accordingly, the telegram from the King's representative remained unanswered. He was absolutely at war with humanity, aged and embittered by continual disappointment and his long struggle for recognition.

And now, his creditors having got on his trail again, began to press for payment. Life has become unbearable: he must find some new hiding-place. His friend Weissheimer advises him to go to Rauhen Alb, a secluded spot, far from the railway.

Once more the poor musician packs his shabby trunks: once more he must seek ... but at this moment a visiting-card is handed to him:

"Von Pfistermeister, *Secretaire aulique de S. M. le roi de Bavière*".

Wagner, who had often enough been disappointed by visiting-cards of this kind, refuses to see the visitor. Pfistermeister however, will not be refused admittance and requests in the King's name for an interview. Reluctantly it is granted and Weissheimer, Wagner's good friend, leaves the room to wait in trepidation outside, listening to the Statesman, who with great powers of persuasion attempts to allay the composer's suspicions. At last the interview draws to its close: Weissheimer reenters the room and Wagner, weeping, falls on his neck, overcome with joy:

"Oh, Weissheimer! I can hardly believe it is meant for me—and that it should come today, of all days! Send away the carriage!——Instead of to Rauhen Alb I am bidden to the King at Munich to-morrow! To this man —*this* man!"

As he speaks he keeps on pointing to a photograph of Ludwig II., magnificently framed, upon which lies a diamond ring. "*Und Winterstürme wichen dem Wonnemond!*" ("And stormy winter melted in moon of spring!")

*

At the castle the King waits and waits——

At last Pfistermeister appears with the glad news:

"He has come and will stay!"

The King is beside himself with joy and remains hours alone in his study, preparing for the long-awaited visit. No one is to disturb him. Before his mind's eye he paints the picture of the great creator of *Lohengrin*: tall, majestic, proud, with a deep voice, sensitive as an actor, eccentric as is every genius.

And in the afternoon of the 4th May 1864 the man himself with all his short-comings, stood before him: a man with legs too short, features too prominent, a head too large, with a care-worn look in his eyes and a strong Saxon dialect ! This 51-year-old insignificant looking man bowed low over the hand of the nineteen-year-old, distinguished looking young King, in his magnificent study.

For one moment the King's youthful enthusiasm ebbed low, for never had he imagined the writer of *Lohengrin* to be thus. He had imagined himself taking the great poet and composer in his arms with the words: "At last ! My wonderful Wagner !"——and suddenly the words died away on his lips !

Wagner, for his part, could only stammer his thanks over and over again, bending over the King's hand. The silence remained still unbroken, till a strange thought flashed through the King's mind: "This is the tragedy of my discipleship ! For me this is the parting of the ways". The King was the first to speak:

"You are the man I have sought for, you are a Master, who can give men happiness. You alone can guide me to the lonely summits, far from all earthly cares. I understand you, your verse, your music: from the depths of my being I feel drawn to you in mind and spirit, Master of divine song !"

"Till now, Your Majesty, no man has understood me. Either they will not or they cannot understand. Up till now my lot has been disappointment and humiliation, hunger, misery and discord at home. One thing alone remains untouched, my poems in music, which I beg Your Majesty to graciously consider."

"To consider? Why, I have studied not only them but you yourself through their medium. Lohengrin alone is a wealth of beauty with its heavenly Swan-song. And if none other will understand you, Meister Wagner, I, your King, have found you and will build around you a stronghold, within whose silent walls we will, together, create the Art of the Future, to be the joy of generations unborn."

The King, in the fullness of his heart, was carried away in a fit of blind enthusiasm to speak as a Lohengrin might have spoken. And the scales falling from his eyes, he recognizes the man in the velvet jacket and cap for what he really is: the sensitively chiselled face with its finely arched nose and the two burning eyes, speak to him of the great soul within.

Wagner remains silent: he is too overpowered for words. At last he says:

"Your Majesty! I can hardly believe that I have at last found someone who so absolutely identifies himself with my thoughts and wishes. A mighty ocean of sound roars in my ears: figures clamour for recognition and for re-birth whose names live only in the great legends of our land. Over all I see in my mind's eye a temple radiant with light, wherein the German Art of the Future shall be crowned. This temple must excel in every respect, putting all our other opera-houses to shame. But what am I saying——forgive me; these are castles in the air, Your Majesty, Utopia nothing else, but a Utopia which I build day and night, not even stopping when I am in Your Majesty's presence !"

"Utopia ? What you say can become reality. I am a King. It lies in my power to realize all your dreams. Why not ? I am young and can do a great deal if I wish !"

Wagner went down again on his knee before his King.

"Don't kneel, *Meister*, but come with me."

Together they traversed several rooms furnished in gold until they reached a smaller, pale-blue room where the King led his friend towards a grand-piano, saying:

"Play me something from your *Lohengrin*."

And the *Meister* played, his finely-formed hands drawing dramatic pictures of that great opera. Before the King's eyes arose those scenes, which, as a fifteen-year-old Prince had so much moved him. As Wagner continued playing, dreamily, it seemed to the solitary listener that in the full, deep chords and haunting themes, he could see the thread of connection between this tragedy of genius and the fate the composer.

The rejection of his earlier works had opened Wagner's eyes to his isolation as an artist. The impossibility of reconciling his true calling with the demands of ordinary life, had found its expression in *Lohengrin*. Lohengrin's ardent desire for Elsa is unquenchable, yet he cannot

29

raise her to the level of the immortals without losing his own immortality. So Wagner himself can never be understood by the general public without prostituting his art. His only alternative is to take refuge in his Montsalvat,—in isolation.

When Wagner stopped playing, the King's eyes were full of tears.

"We will build ourselves this Montsalvat, *Meister*! I give you my word, my royal word of honour that the temple of stainless art shall arise! But I want you to remain with me, to work, to rest and to produce your great works here. All that you need shall be put at your disposal. Here you shall finish the '*Nibelungen*' and I will have it produced. You shall be absolutely your own master, not simply a conductor."

The King had spoken with the eagerness of a child. Dizzy with joy the composer left the Palace, hardly able to believe his senses.

Was it pure chance that this man should cross the path of one of the most altruistic art-patrons amongst German Princes, or were these two men preordained by the laws of nature to meet, each supplementing the other in their mutual striving towards the same high goal?

*

Up till now Wagner had lived in the most complete seclusion, but now his mode of life underwent a great change. The creditors in Vienna were payed off and arrangements were set on foot to move his entire household to a house on the shores of Starnberg lake, formerly the country residence of the Pellet family, which was rented for his use.

Almost every day the royal carriage fetched him to the castle in the neighbouring village of Berg, to confer with the King. There, in the somewhat melancholy-looking grounds of the Kings summer-residence, on the east shore of the lake they sat, frequently for hours at a time, talking and planning how they should set Wagner's works in the spot-light of the world.

Meanwhile, however, at the Court in Munich jealousy, like a poison-snake glides in, finding with ghastly instinct a hiding-place at the very foot of the throne.

Wagner, as man of the world, was the first to sense danger and writes to his friend Weissheimer in Stuttgart the following fateful words:

> "The young King is unfortunately so handsome, a man of such fine sensibilities and splendid character that I fear his life is doomed to fade like a day-dream at the first contact with this cruel world."

To jealousy came also lack of understanding on the part of many leading persons in the State, as the great motive force. The King, noticing none of all this prepared, as a sort of foretaste of what was to follow, a special festival-production of the *Fliegender Holländer*, which was to be followed by *Tristan* and as culmination by the *Ring der Nibelungen*.

It was at the beginning of October of this same year that Wagner left Starnberg to take up his residence in

Munich, in a furnished villa, placed at his disposal by his patron, at 21 Brienner Street. From this time onwards, he was to receive a very considerable salary. Wagner, who after long disastrous years was still very modest, begged that the real sum should not be made known, his salary being given out officially at a lower figure. This he did, knowing human nature and to avoid gossip.

On the 4th December he conducted for the first time a public performance of his *Fliegender Holländer* and had a great ovation. Plans now went forward, by order of His Majesty, to turn the smaller Residence Theatre into a School of Opera, with Wagner at its head, whilst Bavaria's capital was to see the erection of a great new theatre built after Wagner's own design, to house special festival performances. For this purpose, he sent for the architect Semper to come to Munich, whom he presented to the King. (See plate 5.)

It was finally arranged that the site for this magnificent building should be the slope above the Maximilian Park, from whence a broad street should lead down to the Isar, which was to be spanned by a bridge in Renaissance style. Semper estimated the total cost at 5 million Gulden.

The Treasury officials, trained in the reign of Maximilian to extreme economy, raised tremendous objection to the plan. For Ludwig this was the first great blow. Hardly a year had he been Bavaria's king and called too young to the duties of government, was not yet able to parry the blow cleverly enough. Caught in the net of secret intrigues, he was forced to take the advice of his ministers and

Bild 6: König Ludwig II. mit Braut Prinzessin Sophie
King Ludwig II. with his fiancée, the Princess Sophie

to postpone carrying out his magnificent plans for the building — for an indefinite space of time. Later on, in a fit of justifiable anger, he gave up the whole idea, though subsequently the plans were used in a modified form for the Richard Wagner Theatre in Bayreuth.

Whilst the opposition had cut the King personally to the quick, actually it was only directed against Wagner. The nobles were jealous of Wagner seeing in him the revolutionary of former years and as such, judged him to be the young, inexperienced King's evil genius, standing between themselves and the monarch. The priests were against Wagner, knowing him to be a free-thinker, whilst many were the musicians who hated him, seeing in the "Art of the Future" a stumbling-block for themselves. Others again grudged the former revolutionary, until recently up to his eyes in debts, the favouritism shewn to him by the King, holding up to ridicule with cruel cleverness, many of his personal weaknesses.

In spite of all this the young King, unconscious of the intrigues which surrounded him could not bring himself to realize how serious was his position. Having been forced to relinquish the Semper theatre-project, he held all the more faithfully to his friendship for Wagner. Bitterly he wrote to his friend at this time:

"Forgive them, for they know not what they do: they do not realize that for me you mean everything, now and until my dying-day. How hard they make life for us ! But I will not complain for I still have you, my Friend, my *only* friend."

Hans von Bülow was engaged as conductor to relieve Wagner and at the cost of immense trouble they managed to carry out the first production of *Tristan and Isolde*. Till now no theatre had dared to take this risk, but with the well-known singers, Ludwig and Malvina Schnorr from the Dresden opera-house, the production achieved European fame. Without the King's support this success would never have been possible, for he had worked and fought untiringly, putting all his influence behind it. Wagner's triumph was the King's triumph. That a twenty-year-old King had dared opposition, nor furled the sail of his enthusiasm even before the gale of problems confronting the production of such a work of art, this was surely unique in history!

Ludwig, seated with relatives in the Imperial Box, followed the whole opera with the closest attention. The third Act moved him to tears and it is said that the final scene completely unmanned him. One thing, however, was certain: Wagner's genius, in which he alone until now had believed, was a universally established fact.

Jealousy continued and thrived. Day and night secret forces were at work to destroy the friendship between monarch and musician. On the score of "extravagance" everything was remorselessy condemned: it was inexcusable that a young and inexperienced German Prince should be carried away by the fantastic ideas conjured up by the brain of a spendthrift musician. Unrest took hold of the people, of the simple Bavarians, who understood neither the nature of the friendship existing between the King and Wagner, nor the great artistic significance of their mutual aims, for those statesmen responsible for keeping the country informed intentionally neglected their duties. Clever management on the part of the Cabinet brought pressure upon certain circles in the press to take up the matter and to spread poisonous reports. Thus the "Volksbote" wrote:

"In well-informed circles it is no secret that within a year Wagner has cost the country no less than one million nine hundred thousand Gulden, yet Herr von Pfistermeister was unable to prevent His Majesty from making the musician a further grant of forty thousand Gulden."

On the 5 th December Ludwig returned to Munich from Hohenschwangau. On the same day, Prime Minister von der Pfordten presented the King with a memorandum, announcing his resignation unless Wagner left Bavaria immediately, the police being no longer in a position to guarantee the musician's safety.

Prince Karl, the King's great-uncle, feared critical consequences in the near future and servants who were questioned even went so far as to hint at revolution, unless steps were taken to remove Wagner.

This was too much for the King's already shaken state of nerves: it struck to the very roots of his being. The attacks of the Bavarian Parliament, the press, his relatives and of individual Ministers would, however, have availed nothing, had not another influence been at work.

For the first time the royal patron had had unmistakable proof of the intimate connection between his friend Wagner and Frau Cosima von Bülow, wife of the new conductor. The King, wholly unprepared for such news, was wounded in his most vital sensibilities. In his enthusiasm he had put his whole confidence in this one and only friend and had naturally expected the same in return.

After proving the indisputable truth of these reports, he ordered Wagner to leave Munich immediately. That this decision cost him a very severe struggle, there is no doubt, indeed he must have been almost beside himself to have given such an order as he did to his Prime Minister. Yet with his unfailing sense of delicacy he found words to soften the blow for Wagner by pleading the following reason for his decision:

"I must shew my dear people that their confidence and love mean more to me than anything else."

The official letter ordering Wagner to leave Munich was accompanied by a few friendly words, taking the form of a personal request.

This was truly typical of the character of Ludwig II. of Bavaria.

III. Love's Joy and Sorrow.

That a man like Ludwig II., whose beauty of character was combined with an extraordinarily beautiful presence, whose eyes even men found disarming, should have played havoc with the souls of the ladies, is not surprising. It was therefore no wonder that he was the secret admiration of princess and commoner alike.

One of the main questions with which people busied themselves was:

"When will Ludwig II. marry and who will be Bavaria's future Queen?"

In season and out of season there were constant rumours in the newspapers to which the general public added the usual amount of gossip. The people, in their impatience, could hardly wait for their monarch to fall in love.

But how did Ludwig himself feel about these questions? During his youth his father had prevented all association with young girls of his own age. Maximilian himself had had sad experience of women, which was the only justification for such strictness in the upbringing of the Crown Prince.

The consequence of this was that Ludwig looked upon women as belonging to a higher sphere and in his idealistic way had thought of them as angels without wings. Before he became king, he had never known any other woman than his mother. His manner, as young monarch, was exaggeratedly gallant towards women.

It was however, not long before he began to express a different opinion and one day he said to his teacher Döllinger:

"O these women! Even the cleverest of them argues illogically!"

To Richard Wagner he gave utterance to a curiously naïve opinion when he said:

"You don't care for women either, do you? They are so boring!"

And when the *Meister* asked him what was his ideal of what a woman should be like, he got the answer:

"A beautiful soul in a beautiful dress with a voice like music and perfumed with lilies."

"Ah! But that's expecting the impossible, Your Majesty!"

"Well, who wants it! It's just imagination!"——

Later on, when the Minister Bomhard once tried to warn the King against missing any good chances, advising him to choose, if possible, a Protestant wife out of consideration for the large number of Protestant subjects, the King replied evasively:

"Do you really think it so necessary for me to marry? I've no time for marriage: my brother Otto can do that part of it!"

His grandfather was of the same opinion. His grandson should make his choice quietly, after seeing many princesses: he should not bind himself in his early years by an engagement. Things often looked very different later on, than they did at first sight.

*

Three more years went by, and then a change set in suddenly. The wooing began in a quite harmless manner.

On the western shores of the blue Starnberg lake lies the ancient estate of Duke Max, called Possenhofen. In the centre of a large park, full of beech- and oak-spinneys, the old manor lies hidden, in which two lovely sisters were brought up, the one the future Empress Elisabeth of Austria and the other her younger sister Princess Sophie-Charlotte, both of them cousins of the young King of Bavaria. One could see the unmistakable resemblance to Ludwig in both of the Princesses. Elisabeth, nine years his senior, had the same dark, questioning eyes and the same mass of dark curls, while Sophie-Charlotte was rather more of the pretty and charming type, but with the same sensitive, pale face as her cousin Ludwig.——

Often when the young King was spending a few quiet days in his summer residence, Berg Castle, he would send his younger cousin flowers and innocent little notes to the other shore of the lake. But this pretty interchange of greetings suddenly assumed a more earnest character. Ludwig began to dream of her and to long for her company. He took to rowing across the lake to Possenhofen and spending happy harmonious hours with his cousin reading and talking of poetry and art. Sophie-Charlotte, had to play him parts of the Wagner operas which she did extremely well. Meanwhile she succeeded in captivating the man who laid so much stress on outward beauty and on mutual understanding, by her charm and her unfailing taste in dress.

It was Carnival time, 1867. They met at the Court Ball. The Princess wore a Paris ball-dress of silver shimmering material and the costly jewels of her mother. Ludwig was enraptured by her brilliant beauty, though taking pains not to shew her any particular mark of distinction. But in a letter to his brother Otto he no longer calls this cousin Sophie, but his "Elsa". (See plate 6.)

A week later the officers' ball took place, at which Sophie won the prize for beauty. This seemed to make her all the more desirable to Ludwig. He paid her so much attention that those present could not but notice it. He, acclaimed the most handsome of Kings, was in love with the Queen of Beauty: and already the gossips had it that he was going to marry !

Ludwig related enthusiastically:

"Many lovely women were there, but none so beautiful as my cousin Sophie !"

And on the same day he wrote to his brother:

"I can think of nothing else but Elsa. I feel that it will not be long before the sincere and real friendship between us will change to lasting love and I shall want her for my wife."

The young man spent a sleepless night and in the morning——very early——he begs his mother to ask for the hand of the Princess in marriage.

The good Queen-Mother, who had once, during an expedition they had made together to the hunting-box at Blöckenau, hinted that her dearest wish was to see her only and deeply loved son happily married, hurried over to Possenhofen at about seven in the morning, hardly able to contain herself for joy. Once there, she delivered her message frankly, without reservation and quite ignoring the near relationship of the two in question, nor even remotely dreaming of future complications.

At about nine o'clock the King himself arrived to plead his suit, happy in his love and with the confidence of one who has had the way cleared for him of all obstacles.

On the occasion of a banquet at the Court the news was made public, which, in spite of the gossip which had been going about, was still something of a surprise for everyone. And the same evening the King, beaming with happiness, presented himself to his people: in the theatre, accompanied by his mother, he fetched the Princess from her seat by the Duke's side and placed her beside himself in the Royal Box. The whole house broke into spontaneous cheers.

On the 29th January 1867 the engagement of the King of Bavaria with the Princess Sophie-Charlotte was announced officially to both Houses of the Bavarian Parliament, at which the whole country was overjoyed.

But the disaffected still gossiped and still found something to criticize. There were the wise State-fathers, like Minister Bomhard, who would have preferred a Protestant——the braggarts for whom the bringing of a Russian wife of noble blood from Bad Kissingen would have smacked more of adventure——and last not least, those members of the royal household itself, who dreaded the extra trouble and duties involved in a royal wedding, especially as the two former kings had married whilst they were still Crown Princes. Curiously enough, the really trenchant reason for criticism, that of "inbreeding", was the least mentioned of all! For it must not be forgotten that the Princess Sophie's grandmother and the great-grandmother of King Ludwig, belonged to the same House of Hesse; also that the mother of Ludwig I., as also one of his daughters, were both crazy. Furthermore there were tales about King Maximilian himself, who had died so suddenly, whose state of bodily degeneracy was said to baffle description.

*

Meanwhile, throughout the kingdom, magnificent preparations for the royal wedding began. The City of Munich granted 100,000 Gulden for a costly present and the Mint was to issue a special souvenir coin stamped with the busts of the King and his bride. A golden wedding-coach, costing a million Gulden, was built, which can be seen to this day in the Royal Stables Museum in Munich. Suites of rooms were set apart and prepared, for which special furnishings from Paris were personally chosen by Count Castell, who left Munich for the French capital to seek furniture worthy of the future Queen. And for the trousseau, Ludwig himself ordered brocade, patterned with scenes from *Lohengrin*. The women went wild with excitement and art-dealers did a roaring trade in photographs and prints.

Black carriage-horses were brought to the capital: from Lower-Bavaria came a costly team of eight horses and from the Palatinate, the pick of the horses bred at the famous Zweibrücker stables. (See plate 7.)

Wherever they went, the handsome lovers were seen radiant with happiness. The King's gallantry to his lady knew no bounds, and tender attention took the form of expensive and tasteful presents. In all letters to his fiancée, Ludwig calls her "Elsa" and himself "Heinrich". Soon comes the time when he insists on seeing her always quite alone, without her court-ladies. Yet one thing becomes more and more noticeable, he only kisses her on the forehead, never on the lips. Was this perhaps not real love after all ?

A ball was given at this time in honour of the royal lovers at which something happened which set all tongues wagging again. Towards ten o'clock in the evening, the young King, entering the crowded ball-room managed to get alongside Minister Bomhard amongst the dancers and asked him what was the correct time. On hearing that it was ten o'clock he left the ball immediately, without saying adieu to his fiancée and took refuge in the theatre, just in time to enjoy the last act of an opera. This of course was grist to the gossips' mill and the question was bandied about whether love's dream was already over.

One evening later on, Ludwig brings his fiancée the crown from the Treasury, for her to try it on. On this occasion his manner was very strained, so that it was obvious to all present. After he left, the Princess burst into tears exclaiming: "He is only playing with me——he does not love me any longer!"

On the 17th August, Ludwig's fiancée was officially presented to the French Emperor and Empress, who visited the Court at Munich on their way to Salzburg. Shortly afterwards, the royal wedding which had been arranged to take place on the King's birthday, the 25th August, was postponed until the so-called "Maximilian's Day", the 12th October. The reason given was that certain necessary preparations were not yet quite completed, but the Ministers were sceptical, seeing trouble ahead.

The carriage-horses have come, everything is ready and Munich, the place of royal residence, awaits with ill-concealed impatience, its great day. The oldest inhabitants of Munich, generally so hard to please, are full of pleasurable excitement and many are the litres of beer emptied to the health of his young Majesty and his Queen. But as once more a postponement of the wedding until the 28th October is announced, even the simplest begin to suspect that something is wrong.

A rehearsal with the golden wedding-coach, however, was enough to allay suspicion for a time at least and as it rolled through the streets of the capital, drawn by the pedigree black carriage-horses, all doubts were set at rest again.

The summer had flown, Ludwig's formal visits became less and less frequent and——his desperation increased. What had he done?

Full of idealism and young enthusiasm he had been captivated by the outward appearance of a beautiful woman, only to realize later that their souls had nothing in common. Idealism and realism were two very different things.

"When I marry, I want a Queen, a Mother for my country, not an imperious mistress!" said the inexperienced young monarch on one occasion. Such a Queen and Mother he had hoped to give his people in the Princess Sophie. Later he was to discover that his "Elsa" had more talent for being the imperious mistress than for being the model Mother to her lord and her country. The disappointment that this realization brought him was more than he could cope with: his old morbid unsociability returned so that the thought of all the official functions which lay before him assumed alarming and repulsive proportions. Horror gradually took possession of him at the thought of binding himself to a woman for life, by the bondage of marriage. He thought of his friend Wagner, his only true friend, to whom alone until now he had given his complete confidence and love: one after the other the thoughts chased each other through his over-wrought brain, till in sheer desperation he broke down completely in his mother's presence.——

The 1st October dawned, bringing a further postponement of the royal wedding until the 29th November. At the King's expense eight poor Bavarian couples were to receive their marriage dowry on this great day. Meanwhile however, his own love was long since dead.

From day to day, Ludwig's depression increased. Talebearers meanwhile inform Sophie's parents that the King wishes to marry in two years time, that he feels himself unequal to marriage so early in life and wants to enjoy his freedom a little longer. His aide-de-camp, Herr von Sauer, is entrusted with the task of informing the Princess that she would be wise to break off the engagement, which she accordingly did immediately. But Ludwig, filled with remorse for what he has done, tries to make amends for his inhuman treatment by refusing to take her refusal of his suit.

At this point however, the future father-in-law steps in and begs the undecided suitor respectfully either to marry at the end of November or to break off the engagement. He did not wish to intrude his wishes in any way, but on the other hand it was never his intention to force the hand of his daughter upon any one!

This was a terrible blow for Ludwig. He received the news just as he had decided to solve the question himself. That a subject of his should have stepped in and made his own decision, wounded his kingly pride.

Beside himself with anger, he writes these farewell words to his fiancée:

"My beloved Elsa, your cruel father tears us asunder. Ever yours, Heinrich."

But simultaneously he reported to his secretary Düflipp:

"Disaster, which would have been otherwise inevitable, has been averted."

Not long afterwards, when unfavourable rumours about the Princess reached his ears, he had a bust of her removed from the inner-court of the Palace and at the same time another portrait of Sophie on copper was destroyed by acid.

The public learnt the news through the medium of the Court Circular:

"The engagement of his Majesty the King with Princess Sophie is broken off. This has been done by mutual agreement, after realizing the non-existence of that true attachment necessary for happy married life."

Again it was due to the touching consideration of the King, that those Bavarian couples, to whom he had promised their dowry, were not disappointed, nor was their joy clouded on what was to have also been the King's own wedding-day. Each couple received a considerable sum of money. Also amnesties which were usual on such great festivals were duly granted by him on the 29th November.

The good Munich people were terribly disappointed. All their hopes of bringing, by this marriage, new life into the Court, were destroyed. Nobody really quite believed the curiously worded public announcement and in secret gossip was rife.

There is no doubt that to a great extent the King did the right thing in breaking off his engagement, for there was certainly some truth in the tales against the Princess.

47

She was not only vain, but obstinate. So little did she feel either the scandal or the broken engagement that she soon managed to find a substitute in the Duke of Alençon of the House of Orleans, whom she married within the year. In later life she justified Ludwig's course of action when, as a mother of four children, at the age of 42, she had a love-affair with a well-known Munich doctor, which brought with it far-reaching results.

*

Ludwig himself lived down the disappointment of his early years comparatively quickly and the summer of 1868 saw him in Bad Kissingen on the promenade with the Czar and Czaritsa of Russia and their daughter, the Grand Duchess Maria, Ludwig in the role of the gallant admirer. Indeed it almost seemed as if he cherished definite intentions towards the young Grand Duchess, for he had elaborate plans drawn up for a castle built in Russian style, which was presumably intended for the wedding gift.

The simple Bavarian people now transferred their hopes to the Czar's beautiful daughter. But Ludwig still remained awkward in the matter of love-making, seeming incapable of bringing himself to propose without the intervention of his mother, whom he had somewhat alienated. Love for a woman seemed to him to be sheer romanticism, on a par with his love for Wagner's operas, neither more nor less. His love for the Czar's daughter was again only of a platonic nature.

The Czaritsa herself did all in her power to bring the inexperienced young King to the point of proposing. It was therefore with definite intent that she accepted the King's invitation to his summer residence, Berg Castle, expecting there to see the fulfilment of her secret hopes for her daughter.

It was early in the autumn on a wonderful September day when the Czaritsa arrived at the lonely castle at Berg, the entire surroundings of which had been turned into a magnificent park.

Court gardeners from the Palace in Munich, at the King's orders, had been at work for days on the shores of Starnberg lake. The royal palm-houses in Munich as well as the famous Winter-gardens, had been plundered of their rarest exotics. Where the park ran down to the edge of the lake, the splendour of the south was combined for a few days with the glowing colours of the northern autumn. Palm-trees, flowers, and hundreds of flowering shrubs had been transplanted in the lawns behind the castle and from the terrace right down to the water's edge stretched a huge bed of over a thousand roses in every conceivable colour, brought from the little island on the opposite side of the lake. Above, waved gigantic exotic trees weaving sweet-scented spells in the blue morning mists, forming by day a background which was uniquely beautiful. The whole effect was indescribably lovely.

Whilst making the tour of the lake in Ludwig's private steam-launch "Tristan" (see plate 8) a halt was made at

Possenhofen by special request of the Czaritsa, who landed there to congratulate her cousin personally on her coming marriage. Naturally the King could not refuse his guest her request and so it came about that he met his former fiancée for the last time. They spent an hour alone together, during which time they no doubt took the opportunity to discuss frankly what had passed between them. In any case we are told that the visit went off well and that a harmonious "family day" had been spent. Actually, however, Ludwig had watched the last preparations for the marriage at Possenhofen sadly enough and looked forward with morbid expectation to the eve of his ex-fiancée's wedding, for which he had planned an unusual fête. Honourable, generous and pure-minded as the whole character of this man was, he had thought out an evening's entertainment which should serve as wedding-present to his former love, his long farewell to his "Elsa". It was to take the form of illuminations around the lake between Possenhofen and Berg Castle. The evening began quite ordinarily with a banquet in honour of the Czaritsa on the Isle of Roses, finishing later however, with Venetian illuminations which in reality were dedicated to his "Elsa-Sophie".

The people flocked in their thousands, from town and country to the shores of Starnberg that night, and hotels were full to over-flowing. From the tower of Berg Castle waved the Russian and the Bavarian ensigns. The news that there was something new and unusual on foot ran like wild-fire amongst the watchers, something which would transform the hills and vales of this lovely spot as soon as night should fall.

Just as the silver moon-light crested the mountains a flood of illumination flamed up from the sweet-scented Isle of Roses. A rocket, tearing the night-blue sky asunder, gave the signal that the royal party had embarked for Berg Castle, their illuminated boats plainly seen in the broad silver streak left by a search-light, whilst a Munich regimental band played soft music. Suddenly the band was silent, and from the Castle windows floated the voices of the Court Theatre chorus singing the *Brautlied* from *Lohengrin*, followed by the band playing the Wedding-march and the voice of the tenor ringing out across the water in the direction of Possenhofen with the words: *"Im fernen Land, unnahbar Euren Schritten, liegt eine Burg, die Monsalvat genannt!"* ("In distant lands and far from thy dear presence, a castle stands, the ancient Monsalvat.")

The report of a cannon scattered the echoes on all sides and with one accord the castle and its entire surroundings leapt into a blaze of magic lights. "Tristan", the little steam-launch, came to anchor at the landing-stage and to a tumult of cheers from the thousands of onlookers, the King led the Czaritsa through the glowing rose-garden to the Castle.

A few minutes later as they both stepped out onto the balcony, a perfect roar of cannon gave the signal for a display of fireworks such as had never before been seen. First a rocket sprayed the night-sky with brilliance, followed by fire-balls and catherine-wheels in molten fire-fountains. An indescribable enthusiasm took possession of the watching crowds. Again and again the King must acknowledge the never-ending cheers, appearing at the front of the balcony and waving his handkerchief. He seemed like a Prince out of the "Arabian Nights", standing there in the unearthly shimmer of lights, his great height accentuated by the pale-blue and white uniform which showed him in all his manliness.

Softly a cornet blows a distant serenade, dedicated to the ex-fiancée in Possenhofen and from an orchestra hidden in the grounds of the castle, comes a faint echo. Each followed the other, in perfect harmony, though no rehearsal had been held.

But now comes the culmination of the whole evening. Slowly, majestically a column of water begins to rise in the centre of the lake, which suddenly spreads out into a glittering fountain of changing coloured lights, in all the colours of the rainbow to deepest ruby red. At the same moment a gigantic bonfire springs into a blaze in the middle of the lake, from which a cluster of rockets forming the name of the Czaritsa tears shrieking up into the blue night, to the sound of the Russian national anthem. A rain of coloured balls of fire and glittering silver stars falls sputtering back into the water.

Maria Alexandrowna stands spell-bound. Never was such an entertainment offered to her before: it has been the most wonderful day of her life. She can hardly find words in which to express her gratitude and admiration for such a fabulously beautiful entertainment. She retires to a quiet room in the castle, somewhat obviously, where she awaits the expected proposal from her host, for the hand of her daughter.

Ludwig however, stands outside in the grounds, as though turned to stone. He feels the cold night air, yet his eyes are fixedly watching the dying sparks around him, how some are quickly consumed, some glimmer long to grow gradually fainter and fainter till they die and the great stillness of night reigns once again. Was that not symbolical of his dead love? A shudder passed through his great frame: he murmered something with unspeakable resignation as he turned to regain the house, something which sounded like "Elsa-Sophie, it is all over, swallowed up in darkness and solitude——it was only a dream—— Elsa-Sophie!"

Within the castle the Czaritsa waits in vain. A valet announces that the King has retired to his rooms and wishes to be excused. The hopes of the Czaritsa were thus rudely shattered!

In the dead of the night, at the great bow-window in Berg Castle, sits the King in solitude. With fixed eyes, wide-opened in the darkness, he seeks to distinguish the old house at Possenhofen once more. Over there no loving heart goes out to him, for all is over. Only his earliest love, the distant mountains, still keep their ever faithful watch above the dark forest.

The lonely watcher breaks down at last, and burying his face in his hand he sobs aloud:

"No, no! I cannot believe it! She hated my rose-garden, she scolded my beloved peacocks, she disliked my white doves and she laughed at my proud swan. I cannot and I will not believe it. You too, even you, my Elsa-Sophie, were not real, you were only a dream."

*

At the altar next day, the Princess Sophie became the Duchess of Alençon.

Simultaneously the Czaritsa Maria Alexandrowna set out on her return journey through Italy leaving her hopes unfulfilled behind her. She was accompanied as far as Innsbruck by King Ludwig, who then repaired to the castle at Hohenschwangau, which in future he intended to use as his summer residence instead of Berg Castle.

Love's joy and Love's sorrow had been tasted!

IV. The Fulfilment of the Kyffhäuser[1] Prophecy.

It is well-known that the Sixties of last century, were of considerable political significance for the German people. In Prussia Friedrich Wilhelm IV., called "the Romantic", had been succeeded by his brother who later became the Emperor Wilhelm I. In 1862 Bismarck was called to the head of Prussian politics, and, as such, he had only one ideal, that of uniting all the German States under Prussian rule.

At the time of the Schleswig-Holstein question, Bavaria, thanks to Maximilian, had kept aloof and had been able to act as mediator between the parties. After Denmark had been put down there developed that struggle between Austria and Prussia, historically only too well-known. For Bavaria's policy in the question at this time, and for which in 1866 she even resorted to arms, Ludwig can hardly be made responsible. Never had he, the advocate of peace, ever remotely dreamed that such a question could only be solved by bloodshed, he who approved neither militarism nor armament, the foe of everything warlike. Certainly he gave the order, on the 10th May

---

[1] *Kyffhäuser* is a mountain in *Thüringen*. The ancient Kyffhäuser Saga tells that in this mountain the famous Emperor, Friedrich "the Redbeard", who was drowned in Asia-Minor during the crusade in 1190, lay sleeping and would awaken one day to restore the German Empire to her former glory.

1866 to mobilize the Bavarian army, but it was with difficulty that he was persuaded, even as early on as the 22th May, to discuss the military position with one of his ministers at Hohenschwangau Castle, and when the King's signature to the calling out of the *Landsturm* was required, he had disappeared. It took some time before it was realized what he had done. Apparently, directly after the unwelcome conference with his minister, he had, without further preparation, ridden off at a gallop to the station at Biessenhofen, accompanied only by a groom. From there he had taken the train, incognito, via Lindau to Richard Wagner who was at Villa Triebschen near Lucerne, for whose birthday Ludwig wished to be present. Only when the Prime Minister sent an urgent telegram requesting the King's presence, did Ludwig return. His disappearance at this juncture, was taken very seriously amiss by the Bavarian as well as the foreign newspapers. Looked at from a purely human standpoint however, he was justified and his action was excusable, for surely nothing could be more repugnant for a Bavarian king than to see his subjects take up arms against their Prussian brothers. He foresaw the coming struggle and wanted personally to have no part in it. The grievous conflict with Prussia which then ensued, remains as a perpetual reproach in the history of South Germany.

For the King, the thought of "Bavaria against North Germany" was terrible. Consequently he spent only one day in the head-quarters of his army at Bamberg, taking leave of his troops by proclamation and installing

his father's uncle Field-Marshal Prince Karl, as command-
ing officer.

Powerless and inactive, Ludwig was witness of the
defeat of his troops. The loss of the war cost his country
thirty million Gulden.

Peace was proclamed, but a peace which brought Bavaria neither honour nor advantage, a peace which spelt
only dishonour and loss, quite apart from the humilations
which are the inevitable lot of the conquered. Yet what
did this King do, who after all, as commander-in chief
must take reponsibility for everything that took place
against his express wishes ? He decided to make his first
tour of the country, a decision which argued great moral
courage.

And what was the result ? The twenty-one-year-old
was given such an ovation, that he often could hardly save
himself from the enthusiasm of the crowd. His journey
was a triumphal progress and all the German newspapers
were full of pictures of his now world-famous good-looks.
Realizing the circumstances, one can hardly understand
such a complete and sudden change of mood on the part
of the people.

The sane Bavarians were quick to realize how ill
advised they had been in this struggle on the side of
Austria against Prussia, the more so that Austria, in
spite of unconditional promises, made a separate peace
towards the end of the hopeless campain, without consideration either for their ally Bavaria or for the fate of
the South German *Reichsarmee*. And at last the Bavarians

had the chance to demonstrate their devotion to the man who alone had rightly judged the times and had at least taken no active part in this miserable war.

Ludwig came and conquered! Wherever he went he wished to see the wounds and devastation left by a month of war, arranging wherever possible for help and alleviation.

It was a winter journey through the war-zone, through towns and villages embedded in snow and along roads where the drifts lay deep. At every place he visited the streets were black with people and from the throats of young and old, rich and poor, rose the sound of never ending cheers and jubilation. Never was a king given a greater ovation than Ludwig II. on this, his first and his last tour of his country. And whether in Bayreuth, Bamberg or Hof, in Aschaffenburg, Würzburg or Nuremberg,——everywhere he showed the same warmth of manner towards his people, retaining his kindly interest in the most insignificant of his subjects, laying, with his own hand, wreaths on the graves of the fallen and conferring awards on those who had tended the wounded.

In Nuremberg he remained for a week. His residence, the Burgberg, was besieged from early morning until late evening, by dense masses of people who in spite of the bitter cold seemed never to tire of the sight of their wonderful King, nor of the simple, honest look in his eyes. Here there seemed no end to the sound of cheering and here it was that Ludwig himself, noticing pale, careworn faces in the crowd, sent his adjutant to seek the people out, alleviating whenever possible their individual lot. In field-marshal's uniform he held an inspection of the troops on the Ludwigsfeld, himself pinning war-memorial medals to four flags, at which the troops burst spontaneously into ringing cheers.

Yet in spite of the love and devotion shown him by his people and in spite of his promise to repeat his visit, during the whole twenty-two years of his reign Ludwig never again toured his country. Difficulties of all kinds, in other words his Cabinet, subsequently undermined the pleasure he had had, frustrating his plan of a return visit and eventually even driving him to seek seclusion in the solitude of the mountains.

Soon after the conclusion of peace however, something very unexpected happened: the King of Bavaria signed a defensive alliance with Prussia against France. Such an alliance between two states which shortly before had been at war, could not long remain secret "thanks" to the violent agitation of the ecclesiastical faction, who had not, like Bismarck, the welfare of Germany as a whole at heart, but who intentionally harped on the single string of Bavarian nationalism.

Shortly before the opening of the new *Landtag*, the Bavarian Parliament, in the autumn of 1866, the complete change in foreign politics was common knowledge and as Ludwig in his magnificent State-coach drove from the Palace to the *Landtag* building, there was no cheering crowd for the police to keep in check, nor was there any question of his being given an ovation. Every citizen went his way, nor even took the trouble to raise his hand in salute.

This noticeable demonstration of party-feeling, taking the form of oppresive silence, touched the King's sensitive pride to such an extent that he swore, from this time forth, not to show himself in the streets of Munich more than was unavoidable. On the other hand he could not be induced to relinquish the path he had chosen towards Prussia and a German "*Reich*", indeed he held all the more firmly to his new course, which was identical with that of Bismarck.

Shortly after this a new statesman with leanings to Prussia and a friend and admirer of Bismarck, was called to the head of the Bavarian Ministry: Prince Chlodwig zu Hohenlohe. A perfect storm of opposition greeted his election from the entire royal family, the aristocracy and the Catholic priests. The latter particularly refused to acknowledge the supremacy of another State in important religious questions. This laid the foundation for that intense and wide-spread hatred of the Bavarians for everything Prussian.

Hohenlohe was in no way disconcerted by all this opposition and in 1867 issued a public proclamation to the effect that an alliance had been made with Prussia, that a new military-service law would be brought in on the most modern Prussian lines, that schools must be made independent of the Church and that Pius IX. must be opposed should he declare the infallibility of the Pope. This engendered the bitterest feeling against Hohenlohe. Consequently, in the election of 1869 the Ultramontanes gained a considerable majority, which forced the Cabinet to send in its resignation. This the King refused to accept. It was decided to bring in a vote of no-confidence against Hohenlohe, who was as much hated as feared. The King, hoping that the Privy Council would reject this, asked the Princes of the royal family to refrain from voting against the Minister, which was tantamount to voting against him as reigning monarch. With the exception however, of his cousin Duke Karl Theodor, they all voted against Hohenlohe and so against him, the foremost of them being his own brother, Prince Otto ! This circumstance embittered Ludwig more than anything else. For a time, as head of the royal family, he forbade admittance to Court-functions to all his relatives and refused to accept the vote of no-confidence against Hohenlohe, who remained in office. So disaffection in the land spread and waxed powerful.

1870 dawned, bringing with it a critical time for the King's prestige, for Hohenlohe announced in the *Landtag* that a second-class state such as Bavaria could only continue to exist in alliance with a first-class state and that that state was Prussia, under whose leadership in case of war, Bavaria must fight. At this Ludwig's position trembled in the balance, for after all Hohenlohe was the King's mouthpiece. The King's true-German attitude towards Bismarck's policy called forth criticism and disaffection from all sides, with renewed violence. Even the

61

press of the defeated Austrians declared the King to be incapable of ruling, characterizing him and his faith in a united German *Reich* with countless insulting epithets. Thus the "Unica catholica" wrote:

"By his procedure Ludwig II. has thrown the country into a fever of unrest! Unless he changes his course and can be brought to see reason, his crown is in danger."

At last Hohenlohe resigned of his own free will. The King let him go as years before he had let Richard Wagner go, simply to restore order in the country. He decorated him with orders of the highest merit, assuring him of his continued confidence in his political convictions.

Hohenlohe showed himself worthy of this confidence by negociating a strictly private interview between his King and Bismarck in the house of the Court equerry, Count Holnstein, a confidant of Ludwig. Here romance and realism, a pacifist and an advocate of armaments, a royal dreamer and a statesman of iron will stood opposite one another. These two so contrasting personalities, at their historic interview in Graf Holnstein's house forged still more firmly the bond between them, that of their mutual desire to see the union of all German-speaking peoples and of their faith in the glorious future awaiting a united German *Reich*.

At the opening of the *Landtag* on the 17th January 1870 Ludwig said in the King's Speech:

"The country is familiar with the terms of the agreement

I have made with Prussia. True to this alliance, to which I have pledged my royal oath, I am ready if duty calls me, together with my powerful ally to contend for the honour of Germany which is one with that of Bavaria!"

The resignation of Hohenlohe denoted no change in policy but simply a change in personnel, for his successor, Count Brey, held the same opinions as his predecessor. Consequently the bitterest and most virulent attacks continued, on the part of Ultramontanes against King and Cabinet.

The King himself gradually withdrew more and more from the ferment of political feeling in the country, making many expeditions on horseback to his hunting-boxes and living increasingly in seclusion, though keeping up to date with the work which his ministers laid before him.

On the 8th July of this same year he had gone away for six days, accompanied by his equerry Hornig. When starting on this extended journey into the wilds of the Alps he had expressed the wish only to be called back on matters of the most extreme urgency. Did he forsee that war was so near ? For as fate would have it, it was just in those same few days, owing to sudden tension, that the clouds of war gathered threateningly between Prussia and France, so that a messenger on horseback, bearing the most urgent documents, had to be sent to find the King. Ludwig immediately cancelled his trip, returning by the shortest route to Berg Castle on the 15th July, sending the same evening for the Cabinet secretary, Eisenhart.

He was tremendously excited, pacing up and down the great room with the balcony, fully conscious of the enormous responsibility resting upon him and upon him alone, in the next few hours.

It was nearly II o'clock that night before Eisenhart appeared to deliver his report. Foreign affairs of extreme importance were discussed and hour after hour passed by. The King debated and pondered without coming to any definite conclusion. In contrast to his usual faculty of coming to quick decisions, today he seemed unable to see his way clear. Will Prussia really declare war on France ? That was the great question and if she declares war what part must Bavaria play ?

Ludwig, the peace-advocate, the lover of law and order, exclaimed repeatedly:

"Surely there is something we can do to prevent war ?"

"Your Majesty, I see no alternative" was the oft-reiterated, laconic answer of Eisenhart. "A resort to arms seems to me to be unavoidable."

Should war break out, Ludwig's first thought is to ensure the neutrality of Bavaria. Yet as the thought rises he discards it angrily as remiss, for such neutrality might mean the future loss to Bavaria of her independence. Eisenhart himself keeps on stressing this as the inevitable result of choosing neutrality.

The King is lost in deep thought, turning the situation over and over in his mind. Scenes from the middle ages rise before him, pictures that as a boy at Hohenschwangau he had so often admired: of Otto, an ancestor of the

Bild 10 : Zwei Unsterbliche
Two Immortals

House of Wittelsbach, risking his life for the Fatherland, when the Emperor "Friedrich the Red-beard" was in danger, encouraging his brave warriors at the pass of Verona to renewed effort, in the year 1155; of Margrave Luitpold, one hundred and fifty years earlier than this Count Palatine Otto, storming the Norman camp on the Dyle. Or again, in the fourth crusade against the Saracens, the picture of one of the most famous heros, a Duke Ludwig, who was retained as hostage, as a guarantee of peace. Then there was the Emperor Ludwig the Bavarian who won a decisive victory at Ampfing against Friedrich "the Beautiful", later extending the hand of friendship to him in the fortress at Trausnitz; and of the scene at the wedding-turnament of George "the Rich", when the strong Duke Christoph of Munich tilted against Woywoden of Lublin, unseating him and thus breaking for all time the pride of that great boaster.——Thus for seven hundred years the Wittelsbachs had ruled Bavaria and held faith to their devoted subjects. He, Ludwig, scion of this ancient family, he too was made of the same stuff as his ancestors, his heart beat high for his country...

The King, remaining as in a trance, the Cabinet secretary rudely wrests him from his dreams of German heroism, reminding him of the binding nature of the treaty of 1866, whereby Bavaria undertook to fight with and for Prussia at any threat of danger to the Fatherland. This reminder seems to point the way, the only way, to the young monarch: shows him his plain duty to take up arms with one end in view: *Germany* !

Again every step of the way was gone into conscientiously, the discussion continuing the whole night through. Count Berchem was sent for from the Palace and with him the King went over every detail of the ground again, before he finally gave the order to mobilize the army.

He was now committed to a definite political line, andr just as the grey dawn of the 16th July came stealing in, the Bavarian King put his signature to the document which was to affect the whole of Germany, laying the foundation of her future unity; for the alliance of Prussia and Bavaria, the largest of the South German States, eventually led to the union of all states and the founding of the German Empire.

Later, in Munich when Ludwig responded from the window to the cheering crowds below, enthusiasm knew no bounds. Once more Bavaria's sons did homage to their King, assuring him of their confidence. For a time at least all differences of opinion were forgotten in thei mutual anxiety for the common weal.

War with France had now broken out. The Crown Prince of Prussia, spending a night in Munich on his way to the front to take command, attended the festival-performance of *Wallenstein's Lager* given in his honour. At the continous cheering of the full house, the King, suddenly stepping to the front of the Imperial Box with his guest to respond, both princes solemnly shook hands, thus sealing their pact in the presence of many witnesses.

Never before had the devotion of his subjects reached

such a high pitch and never was Ludwig more respected throughout Germany than at this time. But the strain of these days was too much for his weak nerves, the excitement overpowered him. He was not physically capable, like his brother, of taking any active part in the campaign: indeed there were many other representative duties that he was forced, on account of his health, to delegate.

Great German victories followed one another in quick succession, culminating in the battle of Sedan, bringing with it the dawn of the German Empire. As the opinions of leading persons at the head-quarters in Versailles differed considerably on matters of detail and as the King of Prussia showed little desire, until the last moment, to accept an Emperor's crown, so also Ludwig's final decision was only arrived at after much irresolution and under considerable pressure. In judging these events one must not look at the question one-sidedly, as so often is the case. Ludwig deserves no adverse criticism if, as King of Bavaria, he was not ready to acquiesce at once. It was only natural that he should consider the interests of his land, seeking to guarantee a certain amount of independence for his Throne in the rising Empire. Two things must also not be forgotten: the first is that Ludwig, in mobilizing his army immediately, without even waiting for the consent of the Cabinet, rendered Prussia invaluable practical as well as moral support; and the second is, that since 1866 he had never ceased to advocate in the strongest terms in the face of all the South German States, the union of Germany, cleverly diverting his Cabinet away from their dalliance with Austria. These are undeniable facts and are services rendered by him deserving of some reciprocation.

Once more, as so often before in his life, his greatest desire remained unfulfilled, namely the extension of his country's frontiers. After granting him the so-called "Bavarian clause", i. e. certain rights of independence, Bismarck wrote him a long letter in which he pointed out that the King of Prussia could only accept the Imperial Crown at the hand of a Bavarian King. This descendant of the House of Wittelsbach, who counted three Emperors in his ancestry, bowed his proud neck to the inevitable. For him, peace within the borders of a united Germany meant more than anything else. He who was the prototype for all German monarchs could not have forseen the critical times ahead under the young Emperor Wilhelm II., hardly 25 years later, when Luitpold, the Prince Regent would be forced to address to Berlin the warning words: "We are allies, not vassals!"

His long years of bitter struggle against an inflexible system of government, against the aristocracy and the Church and his hard fight for the union of Germany, Ludwig crowned with one last act of greatness, for with his own hand at Hohenschwangau he penned the letter which transformed Germany into an Empire. It was the summons,—dated 30th November 1870—to all German Princes and to the Senate of the three free Hanse towns, to offer to the King of Prussia, as President of the Federation, the title of Emperor of Germany. When the acceptance of all the different governments had been received Prince Luitpold of Bavaria, who was at head-quarters at that time, was sent on behalf of all the States to offer the King of Prussia the Imperial Crown of Germany.

At the right moment in the destiny of Germany, this young monarch had given the right lead. More than once had he endangered his throne opposing violent court-intrigues and undermining the foundations of his delicate constitution, but in the end he remained the moral victor.

The "*Kyffhäuser*" prophecy,—that ancient German saga —had been fulfilled.

V. Recluse and Misanthrope.

There is no doubt that the artistic side of Ludwig's nature as well as his talent for architecture, were inherited from his grandfather, whereas his taste for the romantic came from his father. Whilst his brother Otto as a child possessed a whole army of lead soldiers, was fond of society and later in life interested himself exclusively in hunting and the army, the Crown Prince studied botany, went fishing and adored the mountains, finding his greatest pleasure in solitude. The blue peaks of the Alps fascinated him: the beauty of the alpine solitudes drew him like a magnet all his life long. Teachers and ministers alike never ceased to regret that the characters of the two princes could not be reversed.

The King's inclination to withdraw from society became specially noticeable after he built the Winter-garden in the royal palace in Munich. Here he had set his heart on having a canoe on a little blue lake in a grove of Indian palm-trees, the famous gardens of the Duke of Nassau at Bieberich having fired his desire to create something quite out of the ordinary. To this end the Winter-garden had its own sun and moon and was entered by an arcade which led out of the King's suite of rooms. A dim glow illuminated the water where a swan majestically ruffled his pearly feathers, whilst exotic goldfish chased each other joyously to the twittering of bright-feathered birds from far distant lands. Amongst flowering-bushes, great palms and bay-trees and cypresses towered proudly, the ivy clinging lovingly to many a homelier tree, whilst the branches were bright with the glowing colours of oriental songsters and parrots. But the time to see the garden in all its beauty was at the entrance of the young King. Coloured lights sprang into being, soft music from Wagner's operas sounded through the palm-grove and *Kammersänger* Nachbauer of the Opera-house appeared in silver-shimmering armour as Lohengrin, drawn by the swan in a golden boat, singing as he floated across the lake the famous Swan-song. Here, whether in winter or summer and in the very heart of the capital, the solitary monarch sought refreshment at the hand of Mother Nature herself, secure for a time in his dreams, feeling himself far removed from the haunts of men: at such times he gave full rein to his imagination, feeling himself incorporated in the personality of Lohengrin. Very few were chosen by the King to enter this garden: only the Crown Prince Rudolf who died an early death, with his mother, the Empress Elisabeth of Austria, and the Princess Gisela of Bavaria ever dined with him there. For them he gave a little banquet in the Winter-garden. Otherwise the greatest pleasure he could have was to retire alone to his magic garden when others slept.

This inclination to shun society and to cultivate the romantic side of life found still deeper expression in the much criticized special-performances in the Court Theatre. Not only architecture and literature, but the theatre and even Wagner himself, felt the uplifting influence of Ludwig II. Without his support the Court Theatre could never have attained that high level of excellence which it did during the many years when Baron von Perfall was its world-famous intendant. But as the works of Schiller, Goethe, Grillparzer or other classics came to life again before his eyes, nothing could disturb and infuriate the King more, than to know that he was being watched by the audience, that his coming and going would be the signal for applause or that every movement he made would be followed by opera-glasses, diverting attention from the stage. To be absolutely undisturbed during such performances was everything for him: whereas the knowledge that he was the object of all eyes, broke the thread of his thoughts. Thus the idea occured to him to command special performances at which he should be entirely alone. Some people may find the idea ridiculous, those devoid of artistic perception may even say that it was childish——but for Ludwig II. it meant unalloyed pleasure and it is certain that every real connoisseur will agree with him that there could be nothing more perfect. The first of these command-performances before the King, took place on the 6th May 1872, followed by 207 further performances, until 1885, when expenses had to be cut down. Possart, one of the most famous actors at Court at that time said that in all his forty years on the stage, these hours were the most impressive and unforgettable.

That which at this time stamped Ludwig II. as a royal

recluse was the fact that he fled before the struggles and disappointments of the world more and more often, into the fastnesses of the Alps. From 1870 onwards he held at bay a life which was daily becoming increasingly unbearable and this craving for solitude gained greater hold of him with each year of his life.

The prince, born to a life of ceremonial, hated court and town life. His childhood and youth had been passed in Hohenschwangau to which he now transferred his residence as far as the accomplishment of his daily duties as ruler were concerned, though his Cabinet remained in Munich. This was no passing mood, nor was his increasingly cold, distant manner a mask of affectation put on at will, as many biographers of Ludwig would have us believe, but the natural and irrevocable approach of the ruthless fate awaiting him.

Up at Hohenschwangau he could speak simply with simple people, fearing no criticism: here the enthusiasm of his people never failed to warm his heart: here no Minister raised his eyebrows in involuntary astonishment, nor must he fear the criticism of some great architect to any of his dearly loved building plans. In Hohenschwangau he met with neither disappointment nor opposition, both of which could infuriate him to an alarming extent. How happy he was in his beloved blue uniform of the Knights of St. George (see frontispiece) with Otto and his mother in the lovely country at Elbingealp, or in one of his hunting-boxes! Sometimes he would spend some days at his castle in Schachen, whose Moorish hall with its marvellous oriental splendour he loved so much. (See plate 9.) The thousand voices of nature whispered to him then, treasured tales of his childhood. With what ardour he would seek the rare edelweiss on giddy heights, hearing the distant church-bells below him, each vibration dying on the wind, or lie entranced listening to the throbbing bells of cow-herds grazing on the upland meadows. On horseback he would pierce the solitude of the remote Graswang valley or testing his magnificent horsemanship, would ride up the valley of the Lech, ringed in with majestic peaks. Everywhere his intercourse with the inhabitants was natural and unconstrained: he had an ear for their difficulties, he was open-hearted and openhanded.

The wonderful thing about this man, this favoured mortal, this hermit of the Alps, to whom all personal contact with the town was hateful was, that in the remotest fastnesses of his self-chosen mountain exile he never felt himself solitary or desolate. That happiness which it was not given to him to find in the outer world he sought in the world of literature and many were the whole nights that he spent absorbed in a book. Books compensated him for much that he had perforce to forgo. From philosophical works he accumulated a fund of wisdom which stood him in good stead, historical works developing his inborn talent and making of him an unusually far-seeing historian. But particularly from books of purely artistic value, especially from poetry, his artistic soul drew the inspiration for the triumphs of architecture which he created.

Ludwig's piano-teacher Wanner had declared that the King had absolutely no talent for piano-playing, yet for hours together, in Hohenschwangau, whilst his only friend Wagner, sitting at the piano, wrestled with some new world of thought, some problem of the *Nibelungen* or of his other greatest creation, *Parsifal*, the King would remain beside the composer, wrapped in thought. No word passed between them, Wagner conversing with him through the medium of the music, Ludwig the while absorbed in the vision of that world which together they would rebuild, the long-lost world of pure ideals so perfectly reflected by the landscape from the windows of the castle. (See plate 10.)

Those Munich patriots who had watched with indulgence the artistic as well as the financial help whihc Ludwig had given Wagner and his almost fanatical friendship for the man 32 years his senior, now began to suspect that Wagner, who had taken part in the revolution in Dresden in 1849, was influencing the King politically, instigating him to abdicate, in short that he was the evil genius of those solitary years up in the mountains. To anyone, however, who understands the autocratic and self-willed character of Ludwig II., this assertion is unjustifiable. And he who has followed, even superficially, the further development of the friendship between these two men will agree that after being forced to deprive Wagner of his official appointment, the King's interest in him was less on account of the man himself, who had been sufficiently financed by him and had

furthermore married Frau Cosima von Bülow, than out
of a desire to preserve to the nation the composer's last
great works. Any other interpretation of the connection
between these two is unjustifiable gossip, and if the
King had any evil genius at all it was not Richard Wagner
but the Cabinet itself. The intention to abdicate, which
was actually discussed with Prince Otto in 1873 had its
origin in embarrassment at appearing at Court, due to
his much changed appearance and to his nervous dread
of renewed attacks against his methods of government.

*

The thankless world once left behind him, this royal
recluse never looked back to it. Receptions at the Palace
became less and less frequent, royal guests and military
dignitaries Ludwig eluded by constantly feigning illness.
Nervousness about speaking in public began to assume
unbearable proportions and from being merely shy he
became definitely misanthropic.—

With women, for whom he had never shown more
than a purely friendly interest, he was remarkably reserved. Since his broken engagement he had never spoken
of love, indeed he avoided every mention of it as if he
knew that love for a woman had the power to unhinge
him. The women with whom he associated at this time
were mostly actresses and singers from the *National-
theater* in Munich. To distract his thoughts he would often
send for one or the other of the great artistes, letting them
sing or recite to him. He could be carried away to an

excess of enthusiasm for a masterly, artistic performance, but his praise was for the artist not the person, though most of the ladies misconstrued the King's enthusiasm, falling hopelessly in love with him. Ludwig went through many a painful scene with quite a number of lady-admirers on this account.

The first of these was the graceful, talented Hungarian Lila Bulyowsky, a married woman. This distinguished tragedienne was asked to recite whole scenes from Schiller and Goethe and was even once requested to repeat the *"Parzenlied"* from *Iphigenie* outside the Palace in the *Hofgarten* on a bitter winter's night, for which she was very handsomely compensated. But Bulyowsky, although considerably older than Ludwig, had no idea of her own limitations. She accepted an invitation of Ludwig to the Isle of Roses on Starnberg Lake where she appeared dressed in a diaphanous and entirely transparent gown, to show her charms——as she thought——to their best advantage. In the presence of various valets and servants, this was an extremely embarrassing moment. Again, on the occasion of her appearance in the newly-decorated Palace, she suddenly insisted on being show all the King's personal rooms, cunningly choosing the most remote of these to fall on Ludwig's neck in a quite indescribable access of tenderness. The King, who had the greatest difficulty in escaping from her attentions, rang the bell, calling loudly to the valet: "Mrs. Bulyowsky wishes for her carriage!" With this episode the King's favour was lost to her for ever.

The uneducated and robust manners of the famous singer Therese Mallinger, soon called forth unpleasing comment. The alto, Josefine Scheffsky, suffered a similar fate, though with the melodious sound of her divine voice she could reconcile the King anew, so that she was often invited up to Hohenschwangau Castle and was even allowed to requisition the royal carriage for her own use. But when she began to reciprocate the King's presents by expensive return-presents, even going so far as to pay for one of these out of State money, she too had sealed her own doom.

Another singer was invited to accompany Ludwig in his canoe on the little lake in the Winter-garden at the Palace. (See plate 11.) And what must this foolish lady do ? She fell into the water intentionally to force the King to rescue her, hoping that with her in his arms he would be induced to propose to her. But she had reckoned without her host, for Ludwig ran the canoe ashore and without a single word, turned the dripping lady over to the care of a valet !

Another and even bolder singer went still further. While she was singing the King retired into his private room in the background and lay down on the sofa the better to enjoy the sound of her beautiful voice. The lady in question, misunderstanding this, took the opportunity during the pause to come and seat herself on the edge of the King's sofa. At this Ludwig sprang up angrily, asked her what she meant by such behaviour and a few days later ordered her dismissal from the town.

An actress who appeared for an audition before the King reeking of perfume, found that he had disappeared after her first recitation, giving the order to fumigate the room as soon as she should have left.

The American, Cora Pearl, the eminent elocutionist, who had achieved world-fame by her beauty, applied several times for an audition, which was refused and when she was once more recommended, this time by one of the ministers, the King replied:

"I have no intention of taking a mistress: I am alone and I prefer to remain so!"

Judging by all these incidents, one would imagine tha, Ludwig was a woman-hater all his life. On the contraryt however, with modest, womanly women who knew how to behave, he showed a charm and natural grace of manner. There were for instance, the American sculptress Elisabeth Ney, to whom he sat four times for the only bust made of him during his life-time; and the daughters of Colonel Benzinger who lived near the Lake of Lucerne and many others.

During his long seclusion it was not a man but a woman, who played the chief part in his life. This woman was the Empress Elisabeth of Austria, his own cousin and sister of his exfiancée Sophie. She had access to the King's confidence by her love of horsemanship, which had been Ludwig's hobby for many years until it caused a hernia which forced him to give up his riding. To the Bavarians it seemed very strange that the King's engagement had not in the least influenced the Empress to give up her friendship with her cousin. This made it all the easier to believe that Ludwig had been within his rights in breaking off his engagement, the inference being that otherwise Sophie's sister would not have felt justified in continuing her friendship with him so openly. (See plate 12.)

There is no doubt that Elisabeth was the only woman who ever really fully understood Ludwig, his over-sensitiveness, his love for the romantic and his craving for solitude. The ideal friendship between these two was so firm and true that no other outward bonds could ever separate them. The Empress was not only a beautiful, but an interesting, vivacious woman. She never inter-fered in Bavarian politics and had the same restlessness of mind, the same craving for solitude and the same dread of contact with the masses as her cousin. Later when the King felt himself constrained to withdraw completely from all participation in Court functions and busied himself exclusively in the mountains, putting long-desired plans into execution, Elisabeth was the ideal partner of his dream-world, whom no other woman could have replaced. Nine years his senior and like himself having succeeded to power very early in life——at the age of seventeen——she was autocratic and self-reliant. With her motto: "I can do what I like!", she was a tremendous factor in helping Ludwig to the realiza-tion of his romantic plans.

Later when her cousin was adversely criticized in the Vienna press on account of the great sums of money which Wagner and the King's special command-perfor-

Bild 12: Kaiserin Elisabeth von Oesterreich
Empress Elisabeth of Austria

mances, as well as his building-projects had cost the country, she consoled him saying: "But after all we can do whatever we like." When people dared to openly question whether His Majesty's mind was disordered the Empress reminded him of Hamlet, remarking: "I think that those who are taken to be insane are the only really intelligent people." Whether all this was really good for Ludwig or not, is difficult to say. But in any case her artistic ideas coincided with his and the friendship between them reached such a pitch that in the regular correspondence which they carried on he would call her "dove", while for her he was always the "eagle". In the Hermitage on the Isle of Roses there was a writing-table to which only these two had the key.

Emperors, kings and famous statesmen visited Bavaria without seeing her reigning monarch. Yet when his favourite cousin came from Vienna to Feldafing on Starnberg Lake, Ludwig would pay her his formal visit immediately, receiving return-visits from her at times when he was refusing to see any other human being whatsoever. All his life the world had expected him to feign something with was against his real nature, whilst Elisabeth alone took him for what he really was. She knew what was troubling him and what would help him, knew his inner-nature with its joys and sorrows and in the hours of his most complete solitude she stood by him, hours of perfect mutual harmony, herself the lonliest of all lonely souls!

At five o'clock in the morning, when all else slept,

they two would wander through the gardens on their Isle of Roses. The days too at Hohenschwangau, when the alpine-rose and heavenly blue gentian shone on the upland slopes of the Allgäu Mountains to the tinkle of hidden springs amongst the moss, when the lake-shores clad themselves in golden grasses and in the shadowed pine-forest the black-cock called, those were days of refreshment when they forgot the world and its sadness.

Although in the last years, after 1880, meetings between the King and his lovely cousin became rarer, till the day of his death Ludwig never ceased to adore Elisabeth, constantly sending her magnificent bouquets of roses or bunches of alpine flowers.

"*Es waren zwei Königskinder...*" (They were two royal children...)   *

Many accounts of the way in which Ludwig II. passed his time in his seclusion are exaggerated and highly coloured, the writers having drawn largely on their imagination, but one thing is certain that this recluse-king in his self-chosen seclusion remained the purest type of romanticist, in every sense of the word.

He lived now entirely for himself, often conversing aloud with himself, dissecting and justifying his own decisions and course of action. He continued to rule, doing his whole duty by his people, remaining true to his oath and the constitution, although the Bavarian Patriot-Party and the Bavarian "Nationalists" never dropped their feud with him, nor ceased to blame him for the events of 1870. Consequently from this time onward his rule lacked the personal touch, for his heart was no longer in his work.

In the autumn he spent a few weeks in the Palace in Munich, waiting with hardly concealed impatience for the winter to set in, at which time it was usual for him to go up to the mountains. Once there, the stilly magic of the alpine snows seemed to exercise a strange fascination for him, entirely captivating his senses.

The King had a special carriage built, which could be used also as a sleigh, to which six milk-white horses in beautiful ornamental trappings were harnessed. The coach-body was in ornate Baroque style, the out-riders wearing magnificent uniforms of the same period with white wigs and three-cornered hats, while Ludwig's body-guard, in the same uniform, rode ahead, the snowy track illumined faintly by the light of a flaming torch in the hand of the chief-groom. The horses' hoofs beat a soft, regular accompaniment to the melody of their perfectly tuned sleigh-bells; giant fir-trees formed a guard oj honour when the King's magically beautiful carriage or sleigh set forth from Linderhof Castle to fly through the silent night. For the lonely man, rain with snow-showers, wind and storm was the weather he loved to encounter. Steep rocky pinnacles covered with ice and snow, wild roaring mountain torrents, or the remote solitudes of deep canyons were the haunts he sought. (See plate 13.)

The solitary man would often stand at his study-window in Hohenschwangau staring out into the darkness, towards the blue-black mountains and forests, to whose feet the deeps of the Alpsee lay hidden, restless in the night-wind. Shreds of flying cloud intercepted the stars, except in the east where the costliest jewel of the heavens, Jupiter, the symbol of human wisdom and knowledge shone clear. The thought came to Ludwig of that cry of Schiller's Wallenstein. *"Nacht muss es sein, wo Friedlands Sterne leuchten!"* (The night must come, then shines my guiding star.)

Reading the King's diary one gets the impression that there were times in his life where Ludwig loved animals more than his own fellow-creatures. Only one bird did he dislike and that was the vulture, which for him was the symbol of brutality. His favourite of all was however, the swan and in Hohenschwangau are to be found dozens of representations of swans in every conceivable material and size. In the first of Kaulbach's series of pictures of *Lohengrin* ("The arrival of the swan"), the form of the swan had to be altered many times until the King was satisfied with it. His next favourite after the swan was the falcon, with his broad pinions, his daring and intrepid flight. For him the eagle was the King amongst birds, but there was one he loved above all others, one which charmed him more than even the swan or the falcon or the eagle——and that was the peacock. He considered the peacock to be the masterpiece of the animal world, the essence of perfect beauty and supernatural pride. Was not the way the peacock carried his delicate crown of feathers symbolic of kingly majesty, and the humble adoration of the peahen for her mate, had it not its counterpart in the relation of subjects to their King? And so it came about that Ludwig chose the peacock as an emblem in all the royal castles built during his lifetime. There is hardly a room without its decoration of peacocks, either painted or embroidered, in gold, in silver or in marble and the floor of the Chinese Palace is richly inlaid with a mosaic of peacocks, glittering like jewels.

When the bells of Christmas-tide swept through the valleys of the Schwanengau, and when in the inner palace-court the ice-fringed basin of the frozen *Marienbrunnen* stood silent, Ludwig was as a changed man. No longer he shunned his fellow-creatures but sought them out, showering gifts right and left. For him Christmas was a time of goodwill to all men. In the ante-room stood a casket filled with gifts of jewels and the billiard-room resembled an eastern bazaar with its profusion of brilliant presents.

But what did all this really represent for Ludwig, this satisfying of the Christmas-wishes of those immediately around him? A people must be ruled and although his people were devoted to him, even to a degree that has fallen to the lot of few kings, those whose duty it was to stand by him and support him in his difficult task, failed him utterly.

*

At the height of his powers Ludwig had fled from the world, to seek solace in a solitude more complete than we can conceive of. He had renounced all companionship, turning night into day and day into night, the better to live in the dream-world of his choice. The thought had taken root in his extraordinary imagination that there must be a far-off land where all was silence and sublimity; here he, the royal recluse, would build his castle and reign in sovereign solitude.

To find this imagined land the director of the Bavarian Archives, Franz von Löher, was sent to the Greek Archipelago and the Canary Isles and later to Cyprus and Crete. When in 1875 he failed to find the suitable setting for the King's project, Ludwig was forced to abandon entirely his idea of leaving his country.

Being obliged again, in the winter of this same year, to spend some time in the Palace in Munich, it was remarked how very much he had put on weight, even his face being puffy and of an unnatural waxen pallor. Those in his immediate proximity noted that he was no longer so handsome, his whole manner seemed changed and his speech less clear. Only very few knew at that time that the King had developed the habit of not getting up until after mid-night, dining at 3 a.m., afterwards hurrying out into the darkness and silence of the mountain-valleys, everlatingly fleeing mankind, ever in search of peace of mind. At this time of all others in his life, his in-born love for building increased to a mania!

Very few there were too who knew that already, in

secret, Ludwig in his self-chosen exile, was building in specially selected spots, castles born of his over-strained imagination, — his magic castles.

Half a century brings many changes. We of to-day recapture with difficulty the picture of this man of vivid imagination, this King-recluse. Yet the creations of his almost supernatural imagination remain to us as unchanging landmarks, the wondrous castles set between hill and dale: Neuschwanstein, Linderhof and Herren-chiemsee!

VI. The Wonder-Castle Neu-schwanstein.

In his childhood, Ludwig's favourite toy had always been a box of bricks. At the age of seven with a set of wooden bricks given him by his grandfather, he built a masterly copy of the *Siegestor* (Gate of Victory) and of the Holy Sepulchre, which he illuminated, tending the flame himself in the guise of a nun. When he was eleven he designed plans for a hunting-box to be erected near the Hintersee, the lake beyond Königssee not far from Berchtesgaden. In those early days the likeness between the little Crown Prince and his grandfather was very marked.

Until the age of eighteen he had been kept extremely short of pocket-money. Only a few months after his eighteenth birthday he had at his disposal several millions, enough to be able to carry out even the most fantastic building-plans, had the money been available in cash, so that after his accession his flair for building developed more strongly than ever.

His first architectural essay was the outcome of his enthusiasm for Wagner's music, i.e. the design by the great architect Semper for the *Festspielhaus* in Munich. Opposition however, in press and parliament, induced the King to abandon the project, which was carried out much later in Bayreuth. The same sneers and mockery greeted the young King when he presented the capital with statues of Goethe and Schiller. Only three of his great architectural creations survived the storm of criticism, the Technical School and the Academy of Fine Arts in Renaissance style and the Gothic church at Giesing.

For one of his romantic tendency, the summer-residence at Berg and a hunting-box on the Herzogstand could not be expected to suffice. The castle at Hohenschwangau, built on to by Duke Max, was not large enough for two separate house-holds and it was obvious, right from the beginning that a combined household with his mother would prove to be an impossibility for Ludwig. In honour or Ludwig's nineteenth birthday, the first since his accession, Wagner had written a special march. This was arranged for a military band and was to be played by the combined bands of the three Munich regiments in the court-yard of Hohenschwangau Castle, Wagner himself conducting, to bring homage to his royal friend. The Queen-Mother however, who hated Wagner, put a stop to the whole plan, feigning illness, even going so far as to stay in bed, making it imperative to cancel the musical event entirely. Two days later the King of Prussia, who later became the Emperor of Germany, visited Hohenschwangau, whereat the Queen-Mother recovered at once, herself doing the honours of the ancient castle. This caused an estrangement between mother and son which continued throughout both their lives. Ludwig never forgave his mother for this insult to his friend.

After his disappointment in love the King changed his summer-residence from Berg Castle back to Hohenschwangau. It was plain that here he must have some outlet for his architectural talents and that at Hohenschwangau it would be possible for him to realize his dreams, at least in part.

The idea of a castle which should be called "Neuschwanstein" had been a long-cherished project of the King and before he approached the architect von Riedel on the subject Ludwig had the whole ground-plan mapped out in his mind.

The inspiration for this building was founded on a curious chain of incidents. Maximilian, Ludwig's parsimonious father, had rebuilt the ruin called Schwanstein and made of it the castle of Hohenschwangau, leaving however, two other parts of the original ruin standing on an inaccessible pinnacle opposite Hohenschwangau, untouched. Even as a boy this worried the beauty-loving Crown Prince, who considered these ruins a blight on the landscape. On moonlight nights, looking across towards the Alpsee from his father's castle of Hohenschwangau, he would watch the rippled surface of the lake and listen to the throbbing song of nightingales, hearing the while the roar of hidden waters, like the beat of great wings. He would look up to the ruin on the rocky peak picturing to himself the torrent pouring from behind it, precipitating itself into hidden depths, joining later the tumbling foam of the little river Pöllat. Then his youthful imagination was fired anew with the desire to build a castle upon those heights, a castle with towers and battlements where he, King of a magic realm, should reign undisputed, high and inaccessible, beyond reach of the sound of human voices and where no eye could peer in at the windows. Here in the sunshine birds should sing to him, nor any other sound disturb the stillness save the tumult of wind and rain in forest and ravine.

On the way home one night from a performance at the opera-house in Munich, part of the stage-directions from Wagner's *Rheingold* occupied the King's thoughts to the exclusion of everything else: "At break of day when the grey mists draw away, the summit of the mountain stands out suddenly, clear and in an unearthly night-radiance. With increasing brilliance the first rays of the rising sun illumine the gleaming battlements of a castle standing high on a pinnacle of rock in the background."

So much for Wagner's stage-directions. At this juncture the King's carriage rounded the bend between Füssen and the little village of Hohenschwangau, where the road enters the forest leaving the plain behind. To the left mountains ascend steeply, still shrouded in the mists of dawn. Ghosts of the immortals seemed to hover over him and Ludwig thought to hear the great voice of Wotan singing:

> Accomplished the arduous task!
> On mountain summit
> The haunt of Gods:
> Priceless, proud
> And priestly the house!

Born in trance and in truth,
Work wrought out of my will,
Stark and strong
It stands superb:
Haunt of a heavenly host!

Thanks to Ludwig's vivid imagination the song of Wotan, true also to Wagner's stage-directions, was destined to be immortalized upon the heights once occupied by ruins opposite Hohenschwangau Castle.

*

In the summer of 1868 a surveyor was given the task of finding out whether there were any natural hindrances to the King's plan of building on the rocky peak. There proving to be nothing against the proposition, work was at once begun, the ruins being demolished and the pinnacle itself lowered by blasting, by about 24 feet.

A year later the foundations, which went down about 165 feet into the solid rock being completed, the foundation stone of marble from Untersberg was laid in the presence of only four persons, the King, the architect von Riedel, Quartermaster Büttner and the contractor Herold. Looking up at this immense pile in all its mighty proportions growing out of the sheer rock, one may well question if this be the work of human hands!

Ludwig, who was not only conversant with every conceivable architectural style, but had also a complete mastery of the technical side of his "hobby", took the advice of no builder or architect whatsoever in any important decision relating to the ground-plans. Quite independently he would criticize this or that, making his own alterations down to the minutest details, convincing even experts of his astonishing knowledge and his feeling for form, as well as his good taste. Had he not been born to the throne of Bavaria he would have made one of the greatest architects the nineteenth century had ever seen. His grandfather's taste in architecture was for the classical, his father's for the Gothic, but Ludwig was not influenced by either of them, chosing for Neuschwanstein Romanesque-Byzantine, for Linderhof Rococo and for Herrenchiemsee the style of the French Renaissance. Each castle was an expression of his own personal taste and unique in itself.

During the war with France, work on Neuschwanstein continued, Ludwig spending the greater part of the year alone up at Hohenschwangau, superintending the building. Here he received Bismarck's delegates: here, after the conclusion of peace in 1871 he awaited the visit of the German Emperor and a year later that of the German Crown Prince. Building had long since become his main interest in life.

In August 1873 the great one-storied gateway of yellow Bayreuth sand-stone with its twin towers, was finished. Over the entrance above the sculptured image of a dog was the motto: "*Bei Tag und Nacht die Treue wacht!*" (Fidelity never sleepeth.) (Later, unfortunately the fallacy of this motto was proved, as far as its relation to the King was concerned.)

Full of happy interest in the rapid developement of the new building, Ludwig could now take up his abode in the temporary quarters which had been erected for his use within the precincts, personally superintending the execution of every detail, sometimes remaining on the mountain for weeks at a time. He spurred the workers on unceasingly, until unfortunately, in December 1880, work on the main building had to be suspended for six full months, owing to differences of opinion and difficulties which arose between the persons chiefly concerned in the undertaking. There is no doubt that matters were not as they should have been. Mistakes were made which had to be hushed up for fear they became publicly talked of. That hardly fifty years later it has been found necessary to renew parts of the main structure, is surely a sign that something was wrong at the time of construction and does not speak well for those responsible for it. Indeed, the difficulties which Ludwig encountered at this time can be said to be the beginning of the end, an end which was destined to be catastrophic, for Ludwig seemed fated to connection with people who were secretly working against him, whilst those who really had his interests at heart he dropped.

It was the autumn of 1881 when work was recommenced, this time for seven days a week, for the King could no longer suffer the least interruption, nor would he brook any more interference with his plans. To prevent this, the public was refused entrance, the King trusting no one to see his secrets: in solitude he would finish his work.

So rose the mighty structure, a fortress, a second *Wartburg**), about 3300 ft. high with five stories, and approximately 645 ft. above the valley-bottom. Around the inner court stood three separate edifices: the *Ritterbau*, the *Kemenate* and the *Palas*, the latter being the residential wing of the whole complex. The colossal roof was covered with great plates of copper. (See plate 14.)

In his choice of interior decoration the influences of Ludwig's youth at Hohenschwangau can be plainly traced. In his old home he had been surrounded by romantic pictures and frescos of scenes from the middle ages which he now made use of in different form in this, his first great architectural venture. The Swan- and Nibelungensaga were his first choice. Whereas in Hohenschwangau only three rooms are dedicated to these legends, the remainder being decorated with pictures from the history of Bavaria and of the House of Wittelsbach itself, in Neuschwanstein, the "wonder-castle of his dreams" as he called it, the whole cycle of these symbolic legends is represented in detail. Other frescoes took for their themes the life of the Minnesingers and the indisputable right of kings. The stories are taken not from Wagner's poems but straight from the classics, though in this first castle of Ludwig's the deep inner association existing between him and Wagner is plain to see, as also

---

*) The Wartburg is a castle in Thüringen in Central Germany, famous for the legendary Singers Contests. Within its walls Martin Luther found shelter during the time of his persecution and here he began his translation of the Bible.

the King's very personal participation in the romanticism of the ancient legends. Through the medium of his friendship with the composer a new world had been revealed to him, the world of the Old German sagas which his romantic soul was quick to seize upon. In the decoration of Neuschwanstein, as well as elsewhere in the King's residences, one is constantly reminded of the great influence that Wagner's operas exercised over Ludwig's life.

His imagination as a creative artist gave free scope to the architect in him, enabling him to combine successfully the purely historical with the legendary in decoration. The transitions were thus carried out with the greatest skill, forming a harmonious whole. The pictures themselves show a unique understanding for artistic values, as well as an unusual sense for the purely decorative. So far as possible he made use of Bavarian products in the matter of furnishings, supporting the artistic industries of Munich as no one before him had ever done. Even if only on this account, his country owes a great debt of gratitude to Ludwig II.

Wonderfully thought out were the colour-schemes of each individual room: green and gold for the study, and blue and white (his favourite colours) for the private sitting-room. (See plate 15.) His dressing-room was in tones of violet to represent that moment betwixt dream and reality, whilst his bedroom was decorated in azure-blue and gold. For the dining-room he had chosen wine-

Bild 13: Schlittenfahrt des einsamen Königs

Bild 14 : Die Wunderburg Neuschwanstein
The miraculous Neuschwanstein Castle

red as being symbolic of the material pleasures. All this is truly typical of Ludwig II. and is carried out with that elegance which was his birth-right, for in such matters he was unsurpassed.

In each room the pictures constitute a unit, each story complete in itself. The entire saga of Sigurd greets one on reaching the anteroom on the third floor, according to the Norse version of the Old German Siegfried story. The pictures show the acclaiming of Siegfried who has freed the sleeping Valkyrie from among the flames, his desertion of her later and his subsequent betrayal to death at her behest. In the study the story of *Tannhäuser* tells of heathendom and the austerity of the Church, even for the repentant. The adjoining room, Ludwig's private sitting-room, contains the whole cycle of the *Lohengrin* story, with text from the poem of that name written in the 13th century, whilst his dressing-room is in rather lighter vein, the subject being scenes from the life of the great *Minnesinger Walther von der Vogelweide* and from that of the *Meistersinger Hans Sachs*. The bedroom, in which the recluse spent most of his days however, was reserved for scenes from the story of *Tristan*, whose deep sorrow spoke consolation to Ludwig. This room, in late-Gothic style, is perhaps the most beautiful of all. The ceiling is in exquisite panelling with intricate carving round the canopy bedstead, the inside of which is embroidered with the facet-shaped arms of Bavaria. The washing-stand is in embossed copper on twisted pillars, each topped with a delicate swan in the same metal. Unique is also the water-tap in the form of a silver swan hovering over the basin, bringing crystal-clear water from the Säuling, a stream at least an hour and a half's walk away from the castle. From the balcony there is a magnificent view over the valley of the rushing Pöllat and in the twilight nothing could be more charming than the little bow-window dimly lighted by a blue hanging-lamp. (See plate 16.) The walls of the dining-room are decorated with scenes from the legendary *Singers Contests in the Wartburg*. Here the furniture is particularly exquisite, the velvet cushions and silk curtains as well as the upholstery, being all in wine-red, giving a wonderful sense of harmony and comfort to the whole room. (See plate 17.)

The state reception hall is in Romanesque style, though with a dome reminiscent of a basilica. The general impression is that of a Byzantine building. The walls show scenes from the Old and New Testament. This room is hardly like a throne-room at all, being more like the great hall of a private house in its easy proportions and Byzantine decoration. About 66 ft. long, 39 ft. wide and 42 ft. high, it lends itself as much to great theatrical performances as to affairs of state. The floor consists of one immense mosaic representing the earth and "all that is therein" in the plant- and animal-world. The ceiling is the firmament with the golden sun and out of the dome, which is of an intense night-blue, shine countless stars. The frescoes connect heaven with the earth. Nine white marble steps lead up to where the throne was to stand, which was to be an altar to the divine right of kings, surrounded by six canonized kings, the central figure being that of Christ the Law-giver and King of Kings. A golden chandelier was added after Ludwig's death, while the throne itself, which was designed to be carried out in gold and ivory, was never completed. (See plate 18.)

On reaching the fourth floor of the castle, the first thing that meets ones gaze on entering the ante-room, which is in the form of a colonnade, is a pillar sculptured as a palm-tree with a dragon spitting fire. The erection of this was to a special design of Ludwig's own. On the landing are scenes from the story of Gudrun, part of the Edda. This is however, not identical with the Old German epic of the same name. Wolfram von Eschenbach's poem *Parsifal*, written in 1120, the greatest German literary work of the middle ages, forms material for the decoration of the corridors. This leads us to the great music room with its musicians' gallery, which is the most complete and wonderful replica of the famous hall in the Wartburg, the hall of the Holy Grail, as described by Wolfram von Eschenbach in his immortal poem. From the purely architectural standpoint this hall makes a tremendous impression, especialy seen in the light of early morning, the walls being richly decorated with scenes from Wolfram von Eschenbach's *Parsifal*, by the artist August Spiess, fresco-painter to Ludwig II. The illumination consists of 616 candles hanging in 4 great chandeliers, each holding 54 candles and in six smaller hanging lights. Along each side of the hall stand five bronze-gilt candelabra, richly set with twinkling coloured gems, each holding 25 candles. Here indeed Parsifal reigns supreme! (See plate 19.)

All these pictures epitomize the ideals of kingly honour and of the chivalry of the middle ages. Many will ask what is the underlying reason for so much reiteration and why such a superabundance: what is the connecting thought behind it all? The inner meaning of all these frescoes and Gobelins, made all the more impressive in such a setting, speaks for itself, giving the key to the King's rare fantasy and imagination. In his solitude it was his only pleasure to personally supervise the painting of each picture, each motive of the saga concerned being brought out at its full value after much research and many alterations. The initiated today reads in them as clearly as in a crystal: in the saga of *Sigurd*, his victory over the dragon guarding the gold of the evil spirits and his dash through the flames to rescue the Valkyrie——in the story of *Tannhäuser*, the desire for earthly lusts, regarded by the Church as the unforgivable sin——in the legend of *Lohengrin*, the Redeemer sent from the Holy Grail exhorting in vain to repentance and a return to faith——in *Tristan*, the glorification of chivalry——in the *Singers Contest in the Wartburg*, the power of the nobles and the grand songs of chivalry——in the *Gudrun* saga, the punishment of revengefulness——and in the story of *Parsifal*, the victory over sin and doubt, entitling participation in the Holy Grail and in guarding the chalice containing the Blood of the Redeemer, belief in whom gives everlasting life, robbing death of his power and bringing redemption through abnegation.

*

Thus in Schwangau a gigantic edifice arose, glimmering like a white cloud against the background of mountains, the uniquely beautiful building called "Neuschwanstein". It is a wonderful experience, when the mists of early morning move slowly up the mountain-side to see the castle take gradual shape through the hovering veilsof cloud, a very phantom! It is particularly tragic that "thanks" to the small-minded opposition of a few ministers it never achieved absolute completion, the mighty watch-tower, for instance, included in the original plans, never having been built.

Yet Neuschwanstein remains a marvel of its kind, and quite unique as an architectural achievement, being numbered amongst the sights of the world. It is rare to find a thing of artificial beauty in a setting of rare natural beauty, one with the other in complete harmony, as is the case with Neuschwanstein. True to the precepts of the ancients, Ludwig built his other two great castles in just such chosen spots of special natural beauty, creating his masterpieces for a more beauty-loving generation to come. All the more harshly did fate deal with him that before the completion of his greatest work, his "wonder-castle" Neuschwanstein, he was robbed of happiness and power. Fifteen years he had worked on this inspired creation, to only spend two short years within its walls, being led out of his "Walhalla" as if he were a criminal !

*

Amongst the many who participated in the decorations of Neuschwanstein was the painter August Spiess. He it was of all others who seemed to have the finest perception for the King's ideas. The fine series of pictures from Parsifal in the great music-room are all by him. After studying Wolfram von Eschenbach's works, Ludwig's earlier enthusiasm for Siegfried was replaced by a deeper understanding for Parsifal. The more he became absorbed in the study and comparison of the two heros, the more arresting became the figure of Parsifal. The story of Siegfried was that of earthly gain, whereas Parsifal points to higher things. Whilst being the stronger character of the two, Parsifal teaches the secret of heavenly bliss through complete surrender of self to a higher power. Siegfried gains his victory over the world by virtue of earthly qualities, by force: Parsifal on the contrary, gaining the same victory by humility. The inner significance of this religious problem has been so extraordinarily clearly brought out in his pictures by August Spiess that the King felt the need of giving the painter some special proof of his gratitude.

One evening therefore, Ludwig invited the artist to accompany him into the park on his nightly walk. This was very unusual, as the King disliked company and always went on these walks alone. After a stiff climb in the starlight they reached the *Marienbrücke*, a bridge at a height of about 295 ft. from which one could see in the darkness the faint outlines of the castle. At that moment a hunter's horn was heard and as if by magic the castle suddenly blazed forth in hundreds of lights, bejewelling the night, revealing its swan-like contours, ghostly against the night sky. On the bridge stood the two solitary figures, below roared the foaming torrent of the Pöllat, the spray of its waterfalls glittering as it caught the light. The artist August Spiess, carried away by his enthusiasm at this magically beautiful scene exclaimed:

"Ah ! to be able, like this hurrying water, to go out over all Germany, on, on into the wide world carrying this scene in my memory for ever, spreading and immortalizing the fame of Your Majesty !"

For some moments the King was too moved to speak, content to watch the play of light and shadow over the features of his companion, who in his turn sank into a happy reverie.

Another similar incident was the King's note, on the 15th August 1885, to the *Hofmarschallamt* (Chamberlain's office) ordering the artificial illumination of the Pöllat ravine at the foot of Neuschwanstein. To accomplish this none too easy task, 120 earthenware mugs were fitted up with the necessary zinc plates and carbon cylinders, connected in two series of 60 and distributed at intervals, cunningly hidden behind stones. So well was this arranged that from the castle neither operators nor apparatus could be seen. Rockets and arrangements for

Bengal lights were also placed at strategic points ready for the display.

The King was staying for a few days just at this time, in a little inn in Fernstein, a remote village in Tyrol, taking his meals and spending the evenings in the most natural and unconventional manner, as was his wont, with the simple peasant-owners of the inn. Not until late that night did he start on his long drive home, which led through the little town of Reutte, past the ancient ruins of the fortress known as the Ehrenberger Klause. In the park of Hohenschwangau a short halt was made to rest the horses, the King meanwhile rowing out in the black darkness across the still waters of the Alpsee. It was therefore past two o'clock in the morning as the four-in-hand, bringing him for whom all these illuminations had been arranged, came swinging up to the great entrance of Neuschwanstein. A few moments later, solitary as usual, Ludwig came out onto the balcony. His appearance was the signal for a thousand lights to spring out of the, darkness flashing upon the tumbling waters of the Pöllat spangling the steep sides of the ravine, showing the Marienbrücke like a crown of filigree spanning the night. Gradually the light gathered in intensity as one after the other hundreds of coloured Bengal lights took fire. Rockets soared up, bursting with a sigh of ecstasy in a thousand stars, flinging their sheaves of sparks into the hissing torrent below. No glimmer of light whatsoever showed from the castle windows, for within its darkened walls a restless soul sought peace unto itself. Once more

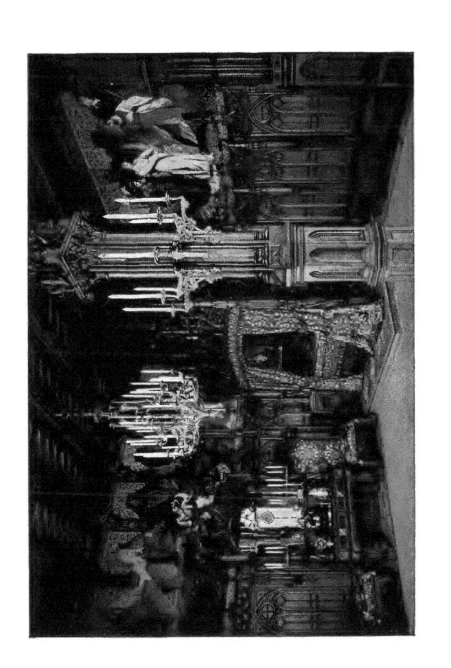

Bilb 17: Schloß Neuschwanstein – Speisezimmer
Neuschwanstein Castle — Private Dining-Room

Bild 19: Schloß Neuschwanstein – Sängersaal (Galerieseite)

in the magic of an "Arabian Night" Ludwig had grasped at temporary forgetfulness, as the grey dawn stole in to lie dreaming of a happier world.

*

Was this man really so solitary in his mountains as one is led to believe? Was he not really surrounded by pleasures of all sorts? Let us put away these doubts as unworthy: let us believe that which 19th century small-mindedness was either incapable of grasping, or else wilfully disbelieved. For surely there was every reason for Ludwig's longing for freedom from a life which had become unbearable, so that he infinitely preferred to live surrounded by the majesty of mountains, than in the dreary desert which the Palace in Munich had become for him who was surrounded by the craft and cunning of jealous statesmen and court officials. Here at Neuschwanstein unspoilt nature was at her grandest, whilst down in the plains jealousy, insincerity and treachery did their worst.

At that time there were those who condemned Neuschwanstein as the ruin and curse of Bavaria. Today even connoisseurs regard this castle as the finest example of any of the royal buildings and the most typically German. With what pride now it is described as being one of the sights of the world. And who shall say how many hundreds of thousands of Marks profit in entrance-fees it has brought in for the Bavarian State! It is enough for us to know that all Ludwig's struggle to achieve his dream has at last found not only a material reward but the reward of immortality.

As intangible as a fairy-story-castle, almost enchanted as it appears, hovering over the ravines, Neuschwanstein now welcomes pilgrims from all over the world, the bequest of a man who was infinitely more than only a king. Looking up at the windows of the home Ludwig so much loved, one almost expects to see him as of yore, gazing out over the landscape, his eye dwelling lingeringly in the depths where still the Pöllat waters roar unceasingly, noting each well-beloved detail on the rocky declivity where the Säuling springs, his gaze resting on the emerald waters of the two distant lakes, his father's castle in the foreground backed by the tumbling torrent of the Lech hurrying down to the rich pastures of Schwanengau.

The great tragedy of this man's life remains the fact that this perfect setting never housed a happy house-party, nor did the rooms ever ring to the laughing voice of a woman. Served in silence, the solitary man spent his days in a world peopled by the spirits of the immortals. With them he held converse, slaking his thirst at the spring of classic wisdom. Meanwhile the bitterest tragedy which can befall a man crept steadily nearer. This house, which for ten years had seen the King's comings and goings, ten years of happy exultance over every sort of architectural problem, was now the silent witness of his farewell. Driven out and desperate, he turned his back for ever to the sweet seclusion which had harboured him and where even death had seemed to beckon to him kindly.

VII. The magic of Linderhof Castle.

Simultaneous with the building of the mighty castle of Neuschwanstein the King had plans under consideration for a country-seat in the depths of the forest, which should form a complete counterpart. As to the sounds of blasting in the valley of the Lech the rock-foundations of Neuschwanstein were thundered out, rose silently higher and higher the outer-walls of Castle Linderhof, in the vale of Graswang.

Here too the whole undertaking had been inspired by an apparently insignificant event, for the adding of a bedroom to an old hunting-lodge ended in the erection of a beautiful villa-like castle surrounded by a huge garden in which were pergolas, grottoes, temples and an artificial water-garden. The King's father Maximilian, had bequeathed his son a simple hunting-lodge about five miles beyond and about 3075 ft. above Ammergau. Certainly the inside was more elaborate than the outside would lead one to expect, being furnished with maplewood furniture, and carried out entirely in blue and white. But so charming as it was, it was no more calculated to satisfy the refined tastes of the son than was the old castle at Hohenschwangau.

Gradually the idea took possession of Ludwig II. to build in the deserted Graswang valley, far removed from civilisation. In sparkling mountain air, in sanctified silence he would set an architectural jewel, gorgeous in every detail; a second Trianon such as Louis XIV. had built himself, should arise out of this forest-land!

The King's idea at first was to build a pavilion with a moderate-sized garden in Renaissance style, the whole to be of quite modest dimensions. He planned for three more rooms, rather better and more elegantly furnished and for servant's quarters in proportion, all of which was to be kept quite simple in style, but it was hardly surprising that he ended by discarding his original plans. For as years went on the love of building proved to be his one real interest in life: his mind was ever evolving plans to adorn his kingdom, to make of it a bequest worthy of unborn generations.

Anxiety reigned in the capital at the high contractor's estimates. Ludwig was made to promise his ministers, who were absolutely devoid of initiative, to be more economical than he had been ever before, as soon as this new wish of his should be fulfilled. After much demur, emissaries were send to Paris and to the Petit Trianon in Versailles to research on behalf of the King, he himself visiting these places three times. After making certain alterations in the design, the King accepted that submitted by Dollmann, under whose superintendence the undertaking was put. Surveyors set to work, the foundation-stone was laid, the gamekeeper's simple lodge serving during construction as architect's office, Ludwig himself taking the greatest interest in every detail connected with the work. He was particularly keen on obtaining books relating to the subject in hand, which he read and discussed with the architects and artists engaged on the building. Not satisfied with his own extensive private library, that of the Palace in Munich and with what the antiquaries in the capital could furnish him, he went further afield in his search for detail, acquiring books of all kinds on the subject of French architecture, the Garden of Versailles, Russian-Byzantine antiquities, the Emperor's palaces, and the Court of Munich during the reign of Karl Albert. Even the famous Book of Ceremonial about coronations and court ceremony was pressed into the service: he must have chapter and verse for everything.

Great difficulty was experienced in bringing the building materials up from Murnau. But the more difficult it became to carry out all his ever varying plans, the more eager Ludwig was to see them materialize. Although possessing the faculty to visualize general effects even before their completion, he deemed it necessary to erect trial-walls at first, which were subsequently enlarged and sometimes even completely demolished, until the effect was decided upon which Ludwig considered to be the most suitable to the site. This of course ran away with enormous sums of money, far in excess of the already high estimates for the building. The result of this was however, that a uniquely artistic masterpiece came into being, meriting the appreciation of generations to come.

"It is to be a Temple of Fame wherein I shall celebrate the memory of Louis XIV." said Ludwig and on this principle he set to work in the wilds of the woods. Ten years later, where formerly forest giants had flourished, stood a charming Rococo palace consisting of ground-floor and one storey with gilt gates, silk wallhangings and gorgeous furniture. In the garden are masterpieces of sculpture in bronze, terraces and pergolas, great fountains flinging their spray to heaven straight out of the rock at the feet of gods in gleaming marbles, all testifying to the vast knowledge of their owner of all that appertained to the culture of the 14th and 15th centuries and to the world of Louis XIV. Surrounded by magnificent country on all sides, this is the only castle of which is was given to Ludwig to see the completion, in the year 1878. Even in this material age one feels, on entering its gates, the spell of its enchantment. (See plate 20.)

On entering, the first thing one sees is an equestrian statue of Ludwig XIV., imperious as a Roman despot. On the ceiling of the entrance is the Bourbon motto: "Nec pluribus impar."

The castle contains ten rooms, one of which, the bedroom, was enlarged three times during the course of building. But the most beautiful of all is the wonderful hall of mirrors, giving the impression of enormous space.

In all the rooms are priceless works of art of every nationality. Some of the furniture is made of rose-wood, the elaborately carved doors and walls rich with gilt, whilst Chinese and Japanese porcelain, majolica and bronzes, as well as the most perfect examples of Meissen china, are to be seen here on gilt console-tables and brackets. Precious stones are used to embellish silver and gilt plates and

dishes and the velvet and silk curtains, door—draperies
and table-covers are richly embroidered in gold. In all the
larger rooms are chandeliers or candelabras of solid gold;
one can say that indeed a heavy toll has been levied upon
the products of a whole world. (See plate 21.)

The mild, flickering light of many candles lends that
glamour to all this magnificence which the King intended.
It was also here that he was able to put into effect a long
cherished desire, that of dining alone at a golden table
which appeared and disappeared at the touch of a switch.
This enabled him to dine unobserved by what he called
"gossiping servants". The idea of this "dumb-waiter"
table was the invention of a French mechanic named Lo-
riot. At such a mechanical table each guest of Louis XIV.
dined: he had only to write the desired dishes on a tablet,
lay this on the table and press a switch, whereat the table
sank into the floor, to return the way it came, set for
dinner with the dishes requested. "Solitary meals are far
better than those taken in indifferent company or with
people one dislikes" said Ludwig one day, though he
never really dined alone, for he set several specially beautiful embroidered chairs around the table for those guests
whom he would have liked to welcome. A servant coming
in saw the King dining in solitary state, but Ludwig who
lived in a world of own thoughts was conversing in
French with his imaginary guests. On his right sat the
Marquise de Pompadour, at his left Madame de Mainte-
non, and opposite him Louis XIV. and Louis XV. From
the walls, well-known personalities of the French court

looked on and took part in the conversation. So Ludwig II. passed his days at Linderhof. (See plate 22.)

*

The whole castle is quite unique in its way, as charming and unusual as the flower-gardens and terraces which surround it. To this day one can see the great jet of water from the fountain rising 165 ft. into the air. Above the cascades is the so-called "Blue Grotto", formed of three grottoes leading one into another. They are however, completely hidden by a great revolving slab of stone which forms the entrance.

These grottoes which were built by the sculptor Dirigl, are a real work of art, being an exact reproduction of the blue grotto at Capri. Not only are they illuminated by a blue light, but have an arrangement by which the illumination can be altered gradually, fading from blue to red, rose, yellow and violet. Although the King had never seen the blue grotto in Capri, he achieved the apparently unachievable in reproducing their structure and light-effects, descriptions in books supporting his own vivid imagination, and his greatest pleasure was to visit the grotto after dark.

As Ludwig entered the grotto, accompanied by his valet, two proud swans floating over the rippled surface of the little lake stretched their white wings, curving their graceful necks. At a signal, the valet passed Ludwig a small golden basket, in which lay pieces of delicate white bread, specially baked for his beloved birds, with which

Bild 20: Schloß Linderhof
Linderhof Castle

Bild 23: Schloß Linderhof — Blaue Grotte — Bild Tannhäuser im Venusberg

Bild 24: Hunding=Hütte

Bild 25 : Einſiedelei

Bild 26 : Schloß Herrenchiemsee mit Latonabrunnen

he fed them. His magnificent shell-shaped canoe, its bow decorated with the figure of Cupid awaited him. Azure—blue light glimmered on the rock-walls, revealing in the background a great picture from *Tannhäuser*, lighted up strangly by the varying blues of light and water, ranging from deepest peacock-blue to palest forget-me-not, mingling magically in the lake-waters with the silver shimmer of the shell-canoe itself. Here, for minutes at a time the King would stay watching through an opera-glass the kaleidoscopic play of changing colours which now followed.

At a second signal—no word was spoken—the valet would step into the little skiff, rowing the King gently over the tiny artificial wavelets. Immediately the azure-blue changed to deepest glowing purple, at first almost dark. The effect resembled that of the midnight-sun in arctic regions, lending the gleam of an unnatural day-light to the surrounding rocks. Gradually this changed to the tenderest rose of dawning day, the rocky cavern-side with its dripping stalactites glowing in the warm light. Ludwig sat spellbound and silent on the coral-red cushions of his canoe, watching the changing effects on the picture in the background, the divine proportions of the *Venusberg* towering behind, in front the play of water-nymphs and gods of love. Tannhäuser, his senses enchained, lies in abandonment at the feet of the Godess of Love, enthroned in all the seductive charm of her divine woman-hood.

A few minutes later all was changed once more. Deep—

green transformed the scene to a cavern in the depths of the forest, rays of light stealing down between the rocky clefts of the ravine-sides with the promise of coming day. A gentle whisper as of falling water was heard, coming nearer and nearer, echoing around the rock-cavern, suddenly breaking in foam from the heights, precipitating itself as a silver waterfall to join the waiting waters of the lake. At this moment to the King's great delight, the swans took wing, circling around his head, their white pinions catching the light till they looked like sculptured silver. (See plate 23.)

Now the waterfall pours from a ruby-red cleft in the rock, the grotto itself flooded in a golden glow. The moving water changes to molten gold, gradually freezing to a white ice-column: day's glowing gold has given place to winter's white. The swans sink back, settling on the water at Ludwig's feet, preening their ruffled feathers, while a rainbow of colours plays over them. These gradually gather in all their prismatic beauty arched over the *Venusberg*, shining like the *Rheingold* bridge whereon the gods took their way to earth and back to Walhalla.

As the play of colour fades away, the King awakes from his dream, the spell is over . . .

It fell to the lot of few people, even amongst those in the inner-circle around Ludwig, to enter the Blue Grotto as his guest. He planned here to perform the first part of *Tannhäuser*, as being an eminently suitable setting for the opera, but gross gossip in the press and public opinion in general being hostile induced him to reluctantly renounce the idea, particularly as it would have involved great numbers of participants and considerable expense. Never was he to see the wonder of the *Hörselberg* transferred to the magic grotto.

*

Near the castle, surrounded by the perfume of massed flowers, stands a lime-tree which is four hundred years old. To the mighty fork of the first branches a little stairway leads up to two benches and a tiny table. This was Ludwig's resort in times of deep depression. The sight of candle-light in the castle windows, the scent of flowers rising from the garden below and the distant sound of the falling fountain, eased his heavy heart. Many a gorgeous dawn upon his beloved mountains, he greeted from this point, those peaks which stood guard around his jewel in the vale of Graswang.

Not satisfied with all the beauty he had gathered round him, Ludwig fulfilled still another heart's desire which was however, less expensive of fulfilment. After much intensive study of Moroccan folk-lore he built, not far from the grotto, a kiosk in Moroccan style, fitted out with sultan's splendour. Many-coloured windows and carpets, a marble fountain, divans and stools set with mother-of-pearl, filled the house. In contrast to the living swans in the grotto, he brought here two marvellous peacocks in bronze set with precious stones. To enhance the whole, the servants wore Moorish garments.

Further in the forest, in the direction of Ammerwald, near the frontier of Tyrol, at Wagner's special request "Hunding's Hut" was erected, exactly reproduced according to stage-directions in the *Walküre*. Here in this primitive wooden hut, in wild romance and silence at the foot of the Geierköpfe and Kreuzspitze, two mighty peaks in this district, the King, with his attendants, spent many a night drinking in old Teutonic style from horn vessels. Again he planned a performance in this Teutonic setting of the first act of Wagner's *Walküre*, but again, for reasons unknown, he was prevented from carrying out his ideas. (See plate 24.)

Not far from Hunding's Hut, in the green twilight of great trees, he built a hermitage, a reproduction of that described by Wagner in his stage-directions for *Parsifal*. This became a favourite resort of Ludwig, when staying at Linderhof Castle. Here was a simple stove for which logs of wood lay ready cut, and here Ludwig, the ruler of all Bavaria, would spend many a winter's night in primitive simplicity tending the fire, intent on some religious-philosophic book, like a penitent monk. Very often too, under the influence of the place, he would read and re-read the text of *Parsifal*, until gradually the desire took hold of him to reproduce every summer the flowering field mentioned in the opera. Accordingly gardeners from the Palace were sent up to produce the required effect, planting grass bepatterned with rarest flowers. The words of Wagner in *Parsifal* were thus realized:

"And never seemed so perfumed, sweet,
The valleys, flower-enamelled.
The scent of all like incense rose
And spoke to me of trustful love."

When the bitter alpine winter forced the hungry deer down to seek food in the valleys, it was one of Ludwig's greatest joys to feed the shy creatures before the door of his hermitage.——(See plate 25.)

During the last years of his life the time spent in Linderhof was the most delightful and held for Ludwig the great attraction of being, of all his castles, the only one which was absolutely complete and just as he had wished it to be. Here the lonely man found some measure of peace and consolation. Perhaps it was that there was more variety in the neighbourhood, perhaps that the winter nights spent in sleighing through the silent vale of Graswang had some quite particular charm for him. Certain it is that that which the peasant no longer notices, taking for granted as belonging to every-day life, the majesty of the mountains, was for Ludwig the breath of his nostrils and became more and more a necessity of life to him.

VIII. The Dream of Herrenchiemsee.

Those who have spent any time on the Isle of Herrenchiemsee know that at the close of a summer's day the
twilight draws a delicate veil of mist across the lake. Such
an evening weaves a spell of dreams over our senses...

Our boat draws to land, we step off into parklands, a
park that seems to speak to us of long ago, telling of times
which saw the new castle arise as a phoenix from the
flames. Climbing the steps leading up to the entrance and
the church, the dream-veil descends upon us:

Erstwhile, on passing the church the monotonous
drone of monks at prayer sounded from out the cloisters
and cells. From the year 764 until 908 they were Benedic-
tine monks and from 1131 till 1803 monks of the Order
of St. Augustine. But then came a change and Herrenchiemsee, which since 1205 had been the seat of a bishop
with influence extending far into Austria was secularized,
passed at first into private hands, later changing owner-
ship continually and just at the moment when a syndicate
of speculators were preparing to clear the island of
timber, the property, in a terribly neglected state, was
bought up by the King of Bavaria, Ludwig II. The first
of the private owners had already turned the church into

a brewery! But now it had passed into the hands of one who would protect and reverence the memory of those dead monks and who had wrested the whole island from the daring hand of the spoiler.

So it came about that this king-recluse conceived the inspired idea of building here a castle which should be unique far and wide. Of course the King's advisers raised every kind of objection, which however, only made the royal architect the more determined, though it lasted eight full years before the plans were ready and work was really begun.

It was not until 1878 that the architect Dollmann was able to start work on the island, work which continued uninterruptedly for seven years. In 1885 the work of building was abandoned, the reason given being that of a lack of funds. Consequently the plans as the King had designed them, were not even approaching completion.

Ludwig had absorbed the artistic ideas of the time of Louis XIV. to such an extent that he now sought to erect a second Versailles, germanized, grander and even more beautiful than the original. Incognito he made several visits to France to gather further inspiration and it was a happy day when first the colony of workmen with their families moved into the model village on the island which had been built to receive them. Day and night three hundred men worked unceasingly to sink the foundations, Ludwig meanwhile enclosing the entire lake-shores from the gaze of the curious. The King would make short visits to see how the work was progressing,

standing at the window of the old monastery watching
the busy crowd of workmen, hearing the thud of spades
and the click of pick-axes. Instinctively his thoughts were
those of "Faust" who says: »*Es wird die Spur von meinen
Erdentagen nicht in Äonen untergehen* !« ("So shall the trace
of these my earthly days, through future aeons never
perish !")

The work done on the island served many purposes.
Not only did it perpetuate Ludwig's memory in the
hearts of all Bavarians, but it became a great asset to the
whole country. Here a second Versailles arose, larger and
more beautifully arranged, and from the landscape point
of view certainly more favourably placed. This building
and its entire decoration is indeed the expression of the
King's own personal taste and characterizes him as no
other castle that he built. (See plate 26.)

The more Ludwig familiarized himself with all that
appertained to the French art of the time of Louis XIV.,
giving free rein to his own tendencies, which were increasingly imperious and absolutist, the more he inclined
to surround himself with those signs of absolutism which
belonged to the 17th and 18th century, synonymous with
the name of Louis XIV. This Bavarian art-enthusiast had
dreamed away the happy years of his youth in surroundings which epitomized court—life of the middle ages. Later
he was to see in Munich many splendid original Rococo
and Baroque buildings, such as for instance the castles
at Schleissheim and Nymphenburg. That he should now
incline to the French style of architecture had its origin

Bild 30: Schloß Herrenchiemsee – Speisezimmer mit dem „Tischlein deck dich" und Meißener Porzellanlüster

in his admiration for royal splendour, for the typically magnificent, and betokened a deeply rooted reverence for bygone days. What caused this enthusiasm of Ludwig —otherwise a true German—for all that was French, particularly for the taste of Louis XIV. who did so much harm to Germany ? This is a very natural question which many will ask.

There is no doubt that the whole idea of this castle at Herrenchiemsee—symbolic of personal royal magnificence as apart from the official royal palace—found its inspiration in Louis XIV., whose son married the daughter of Elector Max Emanuel of Bavaria. For a very long time Ludwig had been inspired by and felt drawn towards the ideals of the great French King. Just as Louis XIV. had disliked living in the capital of his country, continually seeing St. Denis Abbey, where the bones of all French kings were laid to rest, so Ludwig was similarly affected by having to live in Munich within sight of the Theatiner Church, in whose crypt his ancestors were buried. Even the lonliest of us clings to life. Although the three French Kings, Louis XIV., XV. and XVI. remained Ludwig's ideal as far as they stood for the royal and sublime in contrast to the commonplace, as personalities, however, he considered them depraved and from his German standpoint their foreign politics could not find any degree of favour. Was Ludwig immoral like Louis XIV ? Did he rule autocratically like Louis XV., or was he unintelligent like Louis XVI. ? One can safely say that had there been any real affinity between the Bavarian King and the

French it would have been impossible to combine it wtih such boundless enthusiasm for the German chivalry of the middle ages or with the devotion which Ludwig shewed for the so essentially Teutonic music of Richard Wagner.

One thing however, he had in common with the great French King, that neither of them were in the least afraid of spending enormous sums of money on their buildings. It was given to the Frenchman to see the completion of his plans, but the German met with such violent opposition that the north wing of Herrenchiemsee remained incomplete, the south wing and part of the main-back-building were not even begun and much of the interior decoration is unfinished. Such things as the stucco friezes and ceilings, wood-carving and furniture, embroideries, mirrors and chandeliers, nearly all of which were the work of Munich artists, were the means whereby the applied-art studios of Munich first attained their reputation. It is not generally enough known and is worthy of special note that during the reign of Ludwig II. the Munich arts and crafts rose to heights hitherto undreamed of, soon outstripping the achievements of all contemporaries, attaining a European reputation. In the course of his twenty two years reign, Ludwig had spent his royal income which ran into millions of marks as well as a debt of twenty-one million which he left behind him, all on works of art and decoration. On the three royal castles alone, over fifty well-known painters and twenty sculptors were employed. Whilst the grandfather revived and patronized the arts in Germany, Ludwig, the grandson, was the patron-King of the artists themselves.

One hears of a "Louis XIV. or XV. style", and it seems a gross ingratitude that one never hears of a "Ludwig II. style", for Herrenchiemsee is a German king's ideal of what royal architecture should be and one not at all identical with that of the French. Ludwig created a regal architectural style with regal decoration, typifying kingly dignity, with a magnificence worthy of a Louis XIV. These German masterpieces of architecture are not imitations, nor are the pictures in these castles reproductions of those of the 17th and 18th centuries any more than the sculptures can be called copies of the Romanesque or the Gothic. Neither Ludwig's own individualism nor the creative sense of any of the artists employed in the erection of the castle, would have suffered it to become a mere lifeless copy of Versailles, consequently their work has come down to us as a perfect example of the style of their time.

Just as Neuschwanstein, representing German chivalry had been set in the grandest, most romantic alpine surroundings, and Linderhof, typical of the most fastidious aristocratic taste had its setting in a fragrant forest valley, so now Herrenchiemsee Castle began to take shape, a worthy representation of royal magnificence, on an isle looking across lake-waters to a mighty mountain range.

The Hall of Mirrors in Herrenchiemsee has become one of the sights of the world, far exceeding both in size and in decorative beauty that of the famous "galerie des glaces" in Versailles. This immense hall is furnished exclusively with three rows each of 11 hanging chandeliers and two rows of gigantic standing candelabra, accomodating altogether 2300 candles, the marvellous proportions of the hall itself thus being left to produce a tremendous impression of vastness, being approximately 245 ft. long, 36 ft. wide and 42 ft. high. Twenty-seven high, arched windows form one side of the hall, while a corresponding number of tall mirrors cover the opposite wall. The myriads of lights thus produced burned but a few short hours in honour of their solitary owner and his imaginary guests. (See plate 27.)

"Eternity and infinity" was what Ludwig tried to express in the building both of Linderhof Castle and Herrenchiemsee, for he loved to place mirrors exactly opposite one another to produce an effect of infinite depth. With the greatest exactitude these mirrors have been placed with their surfaces vertical, each reflecting the other in never-ending repetition till the eye seems to reach infinity. Yet even this proved to be illusive for Ludwig——he could never gaze into infinity. Between him and what he sought stood his own image, till sight was lost in a darkness beyond piercing. If infinity were beyond reach of his eye, perhaps with the mind's eye he could capture it, for though great enough to endure the immensity of the idea, he showed the still greater capacity of being able to bow to the inevitable, realizing the limits of his human perception.

An impression of space and splendour is created on entering the castle, by the white marble staircase rich with gilt decoration, its marbled walls hung with great pictures by the Mecklenburg artist Ludwig Lesker, symbolic of the nation's life, representing agriculture, the army, commerce, and the arts and sciences, whilst in niches in the walls stand figures by the great sculptor Perron of Apollo, Minerva, Flora and Ceres. The state-bedroom intended for guests is so magnificent that it seems to have come straight out of an impossible fairy-tale, its great four-post bedstead slightly raised like an altar and surrounded by an "impassable" barrier. The bed stands on a purple velvet carpet and is richly embroidered with a pattern of sunbeams in gold. An embroideress named Jörres with twenty women to help her, worked for several years on the embroideries in this state-bedroom, the curtains of which alone being so rich with needlework that they weigh three tons. (See plate 28.)

The King's own bedroom is just as magnificent. The embroidery of the bed itself, in which Ludwig was destined to spend only 25 nights had taken thirty people seven years to complete. Over his wash-stand the gold frame of the mirror is hung with real Brussels lace. As a contrast to the golden guests' room, this room of the King's own is carried out in blues. Stöger, the expert on lighting, spent 18 months experimenting before he succeeded in producing a pure blue light, mild and without any admixture of white rays. This emanates from a great blue glass ball in front of the bed, producing such a magic effect as is only to be found in the Blue Grotto in Linderhof Park. (See plate 29.)

Perhaps the most valuable of all the many wonderful works of art in Herrenchiemsee Castle is to be found in the dining-room, where hangs an immense chandelier of original Meissen porcelain. The model for this was destroyed by special order of the King, after the production of this one example, the King wishing his chandelier to be unique. In this same room is also one of Ludwig's favourite tables, the automatic "dumb-waiter", in gold.

All the sixteen other rooms are elaborate with gilt and Carrara marbles, the detail of all inside-decoration harmonizing with the whole style of the building, its very harmony betraying the individuality of its owner. Herrenchiemsee is a production of unsurpassed beauty and harmony of taste.

Those who to some extent understand the unusual-character of this King will be able to sympathize with the exaltation which he must have felt on seeing the castle of his desires lying before him in all its majesty, worthy of its owner and of its inspiration. Of an imposing immensity, its great front stretches possessively across the island. To Mansard, the French architect, the builder of Versailles, we owe the inspiration for the façade of Herrenchiemsee, that Mansard whose name has only lived in the memory of most of us as the originator of the attic-dwellings called after his name.

It must have been truly a magnificent scene at those times when Ludwig took up residence at the castle, to see the spray of great fountains rise and fall in whispered converse with the many nymphs and woodland gods of the gardens. At night the whole length of the great edifice blazed with the light of over 2000 candles, playing in a myriad reflections on the gilt furniture and decoration, gleaming in endless repetition from mirror to mirror. One must also take into account the unusual beauty of the surroundings in which the castle is placed to fully realize the influence it exercised upon a man who already inclined to the romantic.

Whenever he came it was invariably past midnight. He was always met near the little railway-station at Stock, not far from Prien, by a gondola rowed by two boatmen in Neapolitan costume. As he ascended the great staircase an intoxicating perfume greeted him from flowers massed together on the landings, bespeaking the spirit of Versailles itself. In the hall of mirrors, gay cavaliers with wigs and swords flitted from window to window, with their ladies in swaying crinolines. From the walls, portraits of well-known figures at the Court of the Bourbon King, looked down on the gay scene. And so the shades of bygone days came and went in Ludwig's lively imagination. Thirstily his senses drank in the beauty of the forest scenery outside the immense windows, through which the moon spilt pools of molten silver on the polished floor, reflections from the moon-burnished surface of the lake—waters. And still the great recluse was searching for an answer to his life's riddle, all aweary for contentment, longing to be able to stay the hand of Time and to use the well-known words from *Faust*: «*Verweile doch——du bist so schön*!» ("Oh ! stay with me——thou art so fair.")

But Ludwig's longing is elusive, unattainable perhaps. What is left for him to achieve: something still more gorgeous? Mixed with the sweetness of his pride in Herrenchiemsee Castle is a drop of rank bitterness, for owing to lack of means his dream is broken, doomed to incompleteness. A certain door within this great edifice remains always shut, for it hides an empty pit, all plaster—bespattered, a yawning wound reminding him of the war waged by him against insuperable opposition. Never can he close his eyes to the tragedy of his genius, nor to the bitterness of the contrast between the real and the ideal!

*

Herrenchiemsee!

Slowly we retrace our steps through the silent park towards the lake-shores. Behind us, dreaming in the twilight, lies the lonely castle.

Our mind seems to throb with the effort to discipher the riddle of a bygone age, our senses benumbed as by some intoxicating influence, for here, in the world's most wonderful castle, of which we Germans are justly proud, the dreams of a solitary man, an idealist, have cast their spell over our spirit.

IX. Bayreuth and its Spirit.

Richard Wagner came to Munich, with as empty pockets as a beggar, to leave the town a year and a half later crowned with fame, full of new ideas and inspirations for the future and in his pocket the sum of 40,000 Gulden from State funds which had been placed at his disposal. Many great German poets and musicians had to suffer and to starve their whole lives long and no one took pity on them. Thanks to the friendship and help that was showered upon Richard Wagner by the King, he was saved from a similar fate, and his close connection with Ludwig served to protect him against the cunning of the envious, against the fanaticism of the Church, the presumption of uneducated critics, the arrogance of politicians and against the ceaseless intrigues of court—life.

After the musician had left Munich the King relinquished the whole idea of erecting a Temple of Arts on the heights of Haidhausen, as designed by the architect Semper. The consequence of this was that the great stream of visitors which such an opera-house would have brought to Munich was diverted elsewhere, a result which is deplored to this day. On the other hand, the expulsion of Wagner ended in the King being driven into solitude.

The breach and resulting estrangement between the two friends did not last long. Although separated, their intimate relationship remained intact. Wagner lived at first in Geneva in complete seclusion, then in Marseilles and lastly at Triebschen near Lucerne. Here he spent the six happiest years of his life, from 1866—1872, free from all pecuniary worries. Here the King paid him a surprise visit on the occasion of Wagner's 53rd birthday, spending the night on the "*Insel der Seligen*". In the face of much opposition he arranged in 1868 for the first performance of *Die Meistersinger von Nürnberg* which Wagner had completed in the meantime, with Bülow as conductor. By special request, Wagner sat through the whole performance at the King's side in the Royal Box. This was a rehabilitation and satisfaction to the musician for the injustices that had formerly been meted out to him and marked the height of his triumph. From the front of the Royal Box, touched and more moved than he had ever been in his life before, he was called and recalled countless times to respond to the overwhelming ovation. After this victory and with reputation re-established Wagner and Ludwig bade farewell to each other for some considerable length of time.

*

In his youth Wagner had made acquaintance with the little town of Bayreuth and it was here in the quiet Frankonian landscape which has a certain charm of its own, far from the smoke of factory chimneys, from the smell and noise of towns and the banalities of the commonplace, that the Temple of German Art was destined to materialize, in the midst of a population that was capable of generous appreciation.

It was in the year 1871 that the citizens of Bayreuth offered the musician, who had so rapidly risen to fame, a present of a building-site which was in every respect suitable. A year later the foundation stone of the Grand Opera-House was laid. The King sent a congratulatory telegram promising his faithful cooperation for the future. This promise was no empty phrase, for in spite of all opposition he supported Wagner's plans in every conceivable way. When, in April, a public subscription-list was opened for funds for the erection of a national Grand Opera-House, the King donated 25,000 Thaler and presented the entire outfit for *Rheingold* and *Walküre*.

Another year drew to a close, bringing with it a financial crisis in Germany and Austria. Banks that had given credit, were no longer able to keep to their contracts. The realization of the Bayreuth project was thus most seriously endangered, the more so as the 900,000 Marks promised by the various patrons had not materialized. The King was therefore forced to step in and fill the breach. Accordingly in February 1874 the managing directors of the Richard Wagner Theatre drew up a contract with the Court Secretary by which the State supplied a loan to the extent of the deficit of 100,000 Marks. Later on the repayment of this loan had to be granted a delay. There followed ten nerve-racking, exhausting years before the plan designed in Munich materialized in Bayreuth.

Ludwig insisted on being present at the dress-rehearsal

of *Rheingold*, to which few people were invited. Incognito, with a night-train, he travelled to Bayreuth leaving the train at signal-box Nr. 61, a short way out of Bayreuth station. Wagner was waiting to welcome him and together they drove to the Hermitage outside the town. Eight years had passed since their last meeting. Each was moved to tears of joy at the reunion, and both had so much to tell that it was 3 a.m. before they parted for the night. In the streets of the little town the inhabitants had gathered, waiting to greet their King, whose arrival had become known.

During the dress-rehearsal of *Rheingold* it was noticed that the acoustics suffered considerably in the almost empty opera-house, so that it was decided to open the doors to the general public for future dress-rehearsals, disappointing though this was for Ludwig. The King was carried away with enthusiasm by the voice of the tenor in *Walküre* and altogether the whole atmosphere of the newly-created "Temple of Art", which marked the fulfilment of one of his most cherished dreams, filled him with a pride and satisfaction which was as complete and unalloyed as anything he had ever experienced.

An hour after the finish of *Götterdämmerung* the King slipped away as unobserved as he had come, for once, a proud and happy man. Arrived at Hohenschwangau he sent a letter of thanks expressing his appreciation in glowing terms and promising to return often to take part in the festivals. After this he let the designs for scenes and costumes be laid before him, suggesting and criticizing with lively interest, very much to the advantage of those responsible for the stage-direction.

A week after Ludwig's visit the *Ring der Nibelungen* was performed for the first time with tremendous success. Instead of the Bavarian King, the old German Emperor, Wilhelm, was present. Wagner was called upon to make a speech at the official opening of the new Grand Opera-House and in speaking of his generous friend and patron, Ludwig II., he said:

"What he has done for me will far outlast my span of life. That which *in* and *through* me he has promoted, is in the interests of a future which will affect all classes and which means far more to us than what is understood by individual and national life. That to which the King aspires is a high level of intellectual culture, the first step towards the greatest achievement of which a nation is capable."

When the first rush of foreign visitors had somewhat abated, Ludwig appeared once more at one of the last performances of this first season, also at midnight, on the 27th August, again met by Wagner at the isolated signal-box outside Bayreuth. Wagner was the only person with whom the King came in contact on the occasion of this visit. For the first time Wagner noticed how ill his royal patron looked, noticed the look of suffering in Ludwig's eyes and began to have some presentiment of the tragic doom hanging over his friend.

The King had forbidden any sort of official welcome, but the people would not be robbed of this pleasure and gave him such an ovation at the close of *Götterdämmerung* as he had never had before. Besides the repeated calls for Ludwig of Bavaria, voices in the cheering crowd were heard calling for the "blacksmith" who had forged the *Nibelungenring*. Ludwig himself applauded enthusiastically, till Wagner made his appearance before the curtain. The musician, with signs of great emotion, spoke as follows:

> "The Festival performances are over. Whether they will ever be repeated, I do not know. They are the outcome of a firm belief in the German nation and carried out in honour of my royal benefactor, His Majesty the King of Bavaria, who has not only been a patron and protector, but a collaborator in the work."

Unfortunately the Festival finished with a deficit of 160,000 Marks. The royal patron paid the greatest part of this himself. He even went further. Wagner's now famous villa in Bayreuth "*Wahnfried*"—which name means "peace from delusions"—the one spot on earth where Wagner had found rest unto his soul, was Ludwig's present to the musician. Symbolic of the mutual gratitude and friendship between the two men is the bust of Ludwig II. which stands before the entrance to Villa *Wahnfried*.

The *Nibelungen* now entered upon a series of triumphs in all the main theatres and opera-houses throughout Germany. The repetition of the Bayreuth Festivals, the constant performances of Wagner's various operas on all the larger stages in the country, as well as the sale of his books in ever-increasing numbers, soon realized for Wagner an income that was nothing short of princely. This spurred the composer on to complete his crowning masterpiece. All that Wagner did was done under the protection and inspiration of Ludwig's friendship and artistic instinct, that King who during his own life-time suffered the privation of never receiving such encouragement and support from his otherwise so devoted subjects for his own personal masterpieces, his great buildings.

Wagner had reached the zenith of his fame. Whilst Munich was giving his *Siegfried* an ovation, he wrote the last line of his final work *Parsifal*, that great legacy which he bequeathed to the German nation. Ludwig, his true benefactor, made a new sacrifice on his friend's behalf when he issued the proclamation:

"I desire that the sacred opera *Parsifal* shall only be performed in Bayreuth and shall not be profaned by unsuitable rendering on any other stage."

Only by this means was it possible to ensure the most sacred of the Wagner masterpieces, for a period of 30 years from unsuitable performance. During the last stages of his work on the score of *Parsifal* Wagner enjoyed Ludwig's very special protection. The latter had accepted the "Protectorate of the Performances in Bayreuth of Richard Wagner's Works", paid Wagner's expenses for an extended holiday in Italy putting his own special railway-carriage at his friend's disposal, besides paying a rent of 5200 Liras for the Villa Angri near

Naples for Wagner's use. For Wagner's birthday Ludwig sent him two black swans called "Parsifal" and "Kundry", as well as some wonderful damask silk draperies.

Ludwig himself however, was unable to be present at any of the 16 performances of *Parsifal*. He was suffering at the time from a kind of inhibition on the score of meeting certain people and dreaded that the German Crown Prince Friedrich, whom he intensely disliked, might be in the audience. It was also not possible to arrange a separate performance of *Parsifal* for the King.

In one of Wagner's last letters to his royal friend, he says:

"I will not write another note, my work is finished. I have carried out my mission successfully: against the attacks of a whole world of adversaries, I have been victorious."

Wagner sought rest from his labours in Venice. On his short annual visits to Bavaria, the King always received him with unaltered affection, but at the close of the year 1882, when Wagner last visited Munich and prepared to go up to the mountains to visit his friend, Ludwig was ill and unable to receive him. The two friends were destined to meet no more!

Hard as had been his struggle for life, Wagner's fight for death was still more bitter. After suffering a long while from the most painful heart-attacks which at that time no doctor could alleviate, at length on the 13th February 1883 he was permitted to pass to the Great Beyond. Born the youngest of eleven children of a poor police official in Leipzig, he died one of the intellectually richest men in the world. He was one of the greatest geniuses of the 19th century, a distinguished philosopher and writer and as composer, the creator of a new dramatic style. Freethinker in his youth, in his old age he became with his *Parsifal* the apostle of Christianity. In awe and reverence, believers and unbelievers, the just and the unjust, bow their heads today before the "Holy Grail".

Thousands of telegrams flew from one end of the world to the other, one of the first of which brought the King the bad news. The shock was so tremendous that it almost seemed as if he had never even remotely considered such a possibility.

"He is dead?" he shouted, and stamped with such force that a tile in the floor cracked across. But the next moment he came to himself, realizing that even the greatest genius must enter into his freedom through the dark Gateway of Death. Pathetically the lonely man murmured: "So far from me!"

The wole nation mourned, but no one was more desolated and despairing than the King. One of his Cabinet ministers was sent to represent the King and to lay a wreath of *Alpenrosen* on the coffin, which was transported from Italy to Bayreuth in accordance with Ludwig's wishes in a special train. Accompanying the coffin came only Wagner's widow and a few of his favourite pupils. At the Bavarian frontier Ludwig's representative joined the train to follow the coffin to the grave-side as a last act of homage on behalf of His Majesty to his friend. The honoured dead passed once more through the town which had harboured him of yore, to his last resting-place at Bayreuth. Over his open grave the flags were lowered, to the sound of the funeral march from *Götterdämmerung*, a worthy escort for his soul.——

Wagner's music which had until now been Ludwig's greatest joy was never heard again in any of his castles, for it reminded him too painfully of his friend. All pianos in the various castles upon which Wagner had played, were shrouded with crape and after every performance of *Parsifal* a mass was celebrated in the castle.——

*

The last of the lesser German potentates of those days is long since dead and practically forgotten, but the name of the Bavarian King, Ludwig II., is still fresh in the memory of the whole world, by reason of his rescue of Richard Wagner, who but for him would have been lost to posterity. With strange prescience Ludwig wrote to Wagner on the 4th August 1865:

"Long after we are both dead, our work will live. It will shine down the vista of the ages, the joy of centuries to come and hearts will beat with a passion of reverence for an art which is divine and enduring."

In the garden of *Wahnfried* lie the mortal remains of the great composer and of his wife, the noble woman who dedicated her life to Wagner's genius and who carried on and preserved to the world the tradition of Bayreuth after his death. The mortality of the body is sometimes hard to accept. Our consolation is the immortality of the work bequeathed by such a genius to the nation and to the whole world. This will ever remain an inspiration to us and a lasting memorial to that tragic recluse-King, to whom we owe the rescue of the great composer and who alone enabled Wagner to rise to the full height of his powers. This leads us by a natural transition back to the spirit of the present-day, which marks for all time the return of the heroic.

X. The Tragedy of Genius.

On the 22th August 1880—the 700th anniversary since the House of Wittelsbach first acceded to the throne of Bavaria—Ludwig issued the following proclamation to his people:

"Among those virtues for which my people are famous, fidelity and devotion are the greatest. Upon the rock of fidelity my throne rests and devotion is the brightest jewel in my crown."

These were heartfelt words which bespoke Ludwig's innermost feelings. They were acclaimed by all with great rejoicings: only he himself remained in solitary isolation. He thought of everybody and of everything to the exclusion of himself. How much he longed for a kindred spirit, but for him fate had destined no *"Marquis Posa"*.

He who at his accession was in the first bloom of his splendid youth, had become an earnest, melancholy man. In the peaceful atmosphere of the mountains his lively imagination had created a world of its own from which he could now no longer escape. For him the Palace in Munich seemed more than ever like a prison and each year—from 1876 till 1883—the time spent in his remote alpine castles was prolonged by one month. Each return to Munich found him either at Seeshaupt or at Peissenberg—stations on the way to the capital—in an agony of indecision whether to proceed thither or to turn back.

Meetings even with those people whom he knew well, were dependent on the King being in the mood to receive visitors. With the architect von Dollmann he only corresponded, although when Ludwig went to Linderhof Castle they both lived under the same roof. Audiences with new ambassadors sometimes suffered such unfortunate delay that occasionally it resulted in international difficulties.

Unavoidable Court functions assumed as dreadful proportions for him as if he were being led to the scaffold. Weeks of agitation passed before he could decide to appear, and then he prepared himself by drinking eight to ten glasses of champagne. He would then seat himself, hidden as far as possible by flowers and table-decoration, and the music he always ordered to be as loud as possible.

This dread of meeting strangers was rendered still worse by an ever-increasing persecution-mania. Certain ministers infused him with a dread of a social-democrat movement which was said to be on the increase; organized attempts on the King's life were even mentioned. Yet in reality, at the time of the 700th anniversary of the Royal House of Wittelsbach, the social-democrats were very moderate, at any rate as long as Ludwig II. was on the throne.

The King's condition however, became much more critical after his last proclamation to the people on the 22th August 1880, for the dearest possessions of a man —love and friendship—were denied to him. His only brother Otto, was detained in Fürstenried Castle near

Starnberg, in a state of hopeless insanity and a complete alienation had entirely severed his relationship with his mother. There only remained the Ministers of his Cabinet.

This King, so beloved by the masses, had always been a thorn in the flesh to certain government officials who had hated him from the start because he had neither taste nor interest for militarism. These men sang the words "God save our King" loudly on all public occasions, but behind his back they deceived him and intrigued against him. First they poisoned public opinion against Wagner, then they urged on the war against Prussia. Yet when the secret offensive and defensive alliance was concluded *with* Prussia, one of this intriguing clique—and he was moreover a parson—quoted in the press the words from the Bible: „*Unglücklich das Land, dessen König noch ein Kind ist*!" ("Unhappy the land whose King is still a child!")

When one reads of the intolerant criticism in the press and of all the other virulent opposition that Ludwig had to put up with, one must say that it must have needed a great deal of self-control to let such incidents pass without their having the effect of destroying all faith in the decency of human-nature. Indeed, when one takes all this into account it is sufficient excuse for the King's flight into the solitudes of the mountains. Had he not taken refuge from the world this good-natured, sensitive man whose whole mode of thought was so typically German, would have succombed under the flood of insult which he had to encounter and would neither have bequeathed us his castles nor Bayreuth.

A Cabinet composed of state-officials, or what Bismarck called "Kleber", carried on the business of government in Munich. Their one idea was to remain in office and to fill all posts that became vacant with party-politicians. No one made any effort to bring Ludwig back to the Palace. On the contrary, that the country had become a sort of "minister-republic" was very convenient for them and they avoided contact with the King as assiduously as he himself avoided calling them in council.

Though the King repeatedly gave orders that immediate steps should be taken to suspend the publication of those papers which brought vicious criticisms of his special opera-performances and his building projects in their columns and that those who spread slanderous insinuations about him personally, poisoning the air with scandal and gossip should be submitted to severe penalties, his ministers paid little attention and no steps were ever seriously taken to carry out his orders.

This state of affairs was what made it possible for wire-pullers in the background to carry on their policy of intrigue, resulting in the attacks on His Majesty becoming more and more presumptions, until one newspaper wrote:

"Nowadays it seems as if any scoundrel thinks he has the right to criticize and insult His Majesty. It almost looks like an organized system of calumniation; as though the idea is to alienate at any price and eventually get rid of the King."

As not even the public prosecutors were willing to interpose, Ludwig was forced to draw his own conclusions: No minister would be received again in private audience, in future all affairs of state being conducted by correspondence, any specially urgent order from the King being transmitted to the Palace by hand by the King's Quartermaster Hesselschwerdt. Even this comparatively harmless arrangement was pointed to later as having been a "sign of lunacy", though it was really only a pathetic effort on his part to vindicate himself. Yet in spite of passing mental indispositions and long fits of intense melancholy, this King never neglected the affairs of state, which were always punctually attended to. It is not true when people maintain that in the last years of his life Ludwig was to a great extent incapable of thinking or of acting logically, that for days or sometimes weeks at a time he was only half conscious, in other words that he was not responsible for his actions. This suggestion is to be sharply repudiated as having no foundation in fact.

The King's written reports and instructions were in the hands of the Cabinet Secretary von Ziegler. But was it the work of a cabinet secretary to procure the royal signature to important government affairs and even to new laws? Was it not rather the duty of each minister, from the very beginning to insist on his right to a personal interview in which to make his departmental report? Failing this concession he should not have merely threatened his resignation—which occasionally did happen—but should have carried the threat to its logical conclusion. This latter however, never took place. Perhaps if ministers had resigned it would have made more impression on Ludwig: in any case the continual friction between himself and his ministers would never have become as acute as it did in the course of years, jeopardizing his reputation and his position. Without active opposition to the existing form of government on the part of the ministers themselves, things were bound to go from bad to worse. Yet when at last von Ziegler refused to be the go-between on behalf of his colleagues and tendered his resignation to his chief, Prime Minister von Lutz in the year 1883, asking to be relieved of his difficult post, that statesman answered in words to this effect:

> "All peculiarities on the part of His Majesty are to be taken into account and simply ignored. No intervention is admissible as long as the King does not endanger the common weal by any act which might be a hindrance to the smooth working of the machinery of government."

*

Richard Wagner had been laid to rest at *Wahnfried*. The building of Linderhof Castle was completed, Neuschwanstein was nearly finished and the castle of Herrenchiemsee still being built, when the King's already difficult position became still more critical owing to a conflict with which he had never reckoned. The cause of this conflict was the already over-burdened state of the government funds. From private sources the King's income was of quite modest proportions, whilst the official-income granted him by the country showed an expenditure of well over 4 million. The various building projects and the annual grant to Bayreuth resulted in a deficit in the government funds, amounting in 1884 to 7½ million. Creditors began to press for payment so that von Riedel the Finance Minister, with the consent of the royal family raised a loan from the Bavarian State Bank which cleared off the whole debt.

But the new year brought a new debt, this time of 6½ million. The Finance Minister, instead of looking round for some means of balancing the budget, which in his state-capacity it was his duty to do, drew public attention to the difficulties which the financial crisis was bringing to the country, throwing the blame openly on the King. To make things still worse for Ludwig, von Riedel mentioned in his report that probably 20—25 million would be really needed to complete the building already begun and to straighten out the finances of the country. To this the King turned a deaf ear, indicating to von Riedel that he had over-stepped the limits of his duties as Finance Minister. Whereupon this „conscientious" von Riedel pretended to be grossly insulted and gave in his resignation. The Cabinet went one better, threatening to resign *en masse* if von Riedel's resignation were accepted.

In this manner the King's hand was forced, the Cabinet playing, as it were, a game of political chess with their monarch. He thus became pitiably entangled in difficulties of all sorts, he, the recluse-idealist, rescuer of Wagner and co-founder of the great German Empire ! And it was in such an atmosphere of continual humiliations that Ludwig's "dream-castles" approached their completion.

Riedel remained in office, but the Cabinet had fallen entirely into disfavour with the King. Remembering the self-reliance and independence of Ludwig II. one can well imagine whither such a state of affairs must inevitably lead.

Between the Cabinet and the King there now ensued a bitter struggle which lasted a whole year. Two scenes from this painful conflict will be enough to give some idea of the tragedy which was in store for the King.

The following conversation took place between the Cabinet Secretary and one of the ministers:

"Can't you see how the King is ruining the royalist capital bequeathed to him by his ancestors ? If he goes on like this much longer there will soon be nothing left of it, either for him or for Bavaria. That's what comes of his thinking he can decide everything alone. He must sometime have his eyes opened to his real position as King of a constitutional country and to his duties to the Empire. Respectfully but very emphatically we shall have to make him realize the fact that he can't go on like this any longer. And this must be done in a way that leaves him in no doubt as to our intentions: that this is neither pretence nor fantasy, but stern necessity. Neither our contemporaries nor history shall be able to reproach us with having simply pandered to royal whims, neglecting our duty to the nation."

"And what if the King still refuses to be convinced?"

"There are ways and means of attaining our end. In the case of his remaining unconvinced, the King would have to be treated like a child. Extreme measures, such as forced abdication and putting him under guardianship would soon open his eyes!"

"But that could only be done by someone who has no affection for him, who is completely out of sympathy with his architectural projects and who even goes so far as to consider him abnormal."

"If that's all, I could mention the names of many who are ready to go to those lengths in the interests of the country!"

Here the conversation ended.

The other scene took place at Neuschwanstein, when Quartermaster Hesselschwerdt was discussing the situation with the King and said:

"Your Majesty knows how devoted the people are to their King and that they value those castles which are already finished: also that the country is beginning to see the value of all that you have done for Wagner. All the more must Your Majesty be extremely careful now not to do anything imprudent which would cause a reversion of feeling in the country, for there are already all sorts of rumours going about. There are said to be certain people who wish to make it known that Your Majesty is—excuse the expression—insane!"

The King smiles grimly. He is not in the least angry as Hesselschwerdt had expected, yet he betrays a certain perplexity and an ill-concealed unrest as he replies:

"Who could those people be? I can't imagine that such people exist or ever will exist."

"Nothing definite has been decided upon, but someday it might come to pass. All I wanted to do was to warn Your Majesty not to succumb to any new temptations." (The King had just been speaking of his newest designs for a castle at Falkenstein.)

"My one desire is that my people shall realize that whatever I have done has not been for my own glorification: that I have aimed at educating my people to love the beautiful and to leave imperishable treasures behind me for the glorification of my country."

At this point the King broke off the conversation, remaining strangely silent all the rest of the evening.

*

The fateful year 1886 dawned. Ludwig, as often before, turned in his financial difficulties to Bismarck, receiving from him the following advice: A bill should be brought before the Bavarian *Landtag* for a grant to cover not only the deficit in the government funds, but to be sufficient for the completion of the royal castles. This advice was doubtless well meant on the part of Bismarck, but it showed that he had not reckoned with the mentality of Munich's government-officials. With a show of conviction these Ministers entered into negotiations with leading members of both Houses of the Bavarian *Landtag*, but instead of bringing in a bill on the subject, the negotiations were kept secret, ending as might have been expected with a report being issued that the application for a grant had met with opposition in all quarters. What had really happened was, that the leaders of the Catholic Party had told Prime Minister von Lutz that they intended to get rid of Ludwig, had no more interest in his doings and would refuse to pay his debts should this be required of them. These men, having decided not to come to the help of their King systematically frustrated every suggestion which was brought forward in his favour. In a parallel case in any other country it would have been enough to bring in a vote of no-confidence in such a Cabinet, but in Bavaria nothing was done at all to remedy such a state of affairs. They just "muddled along", even finding the courage later on to defend their action and to bring in an official accusation of the King !

Money difficulties became more and more critical.

In the spring, rumours got into the papers that the King's mentality, already known to be in a precarious state, was getting worse. Ludwig, on hearing these lying reports, was beside himself and resolved to furnish a personal repudiation of such insults. Contrary therefore, to his usual habit he went for a walk in the middle of the day, stopping to speak a few friendly words to anyone he met. But this had no echo in the press: they in no wise retracted either the sensational news they had trumpeted abroad, nor did they even, as German papers, consider it necessary to insert official denials of the lies which had appeared concerning a German King.

When Schels, a member of the *Landtag*—a man of fearless independence—brought in a proposal to institute a lottery which would have sufficed to easily cover all the building debts, his idea was opposed by both the government and the press as being an "idle suggestion". Discussions on the order of the day were resumed. No one lifted a finger to help the King, though help could have been so easily given.

In a public speech the Finance Minister explained that His Majesty's debts were not the fault of the Government but were simply due to Ludwig's mania for building and to his having been enormously over-charged—not to say cheated—in all directions. This bald statement having been made, no further effort was expended to relieve the situation. Instead of rescuing the King from the clutches of shameless money-makers and bringing them to justice, things were simply allowed to slide and went from bad to worse.

Any normal person would be incensed at such goings-on. When the King, referring to the foregoing events in conversation with the statesman Feilitzsch said: "If this scandalous business doesn't stop soon, I shall be faced with two alternatives: either I must go into voluntary exile or I must commit suicide", people in Munich smiled and called him "insane".

The results of such dilatory methods were that actions were brought against the government and stock-exchange reports from Vienna and Berlin openly discussed the financial crisis in Bavaria. The Jews, more than all

At last the King could put up with all this confusion no longer. In an effort to burst the bonds of party — politics he took refuge in a last resort:

"Either the government is with me and carries out my orders, or it is against me, in which case it must withdraw, to be replaced as soon as possible by a new Cabinet."

This had its effect on the ambitious "place-hunterts": they turned to Bismarck for advice. He gave the very sound advice that they must bring their recluse-King back to a sensible view of things by means of the usual governmental methods. His Majesty accordingly received the following reply, which was nothing less than an ultimatum:

"To avoid bankruptcy, the King must return to the economical methods employed by his royal Father. In the future all further building projects, separate theatre-performances and expensive presents are to be avoided and the strange and costly visits to the alpine castles are to be curtailed. His Majesty is requested to return at once to Munich, to dismiss his personal staff, to receive his Ministers in audience, and to resume his normal public duties."

That this was a last attempt to re-establish normal relationships, was clear, the Cabinet having taken upon itself the onus of having told the reigning monarch bitter home-truths. Was it really done with a genuine hope of coming to some working agreement with a King whom they had long considered to be undesirable, or was it simply a gesture calculated to serve as a justification in the event of subsequent investigations ? Whatever may have been the real motive the attempt coming now in the spring of 1886 came too late and moreover simply had the reverse effect of that intended.

Ludwig was simply beside himsef with anger. He gave orders to his confidant Hesselschwerdt, to drive this "pack" of Ministers out of Munich, to dissolve the Cabinet and to raise a loan of 20 million from Prince Thurn und Taxis, applying for a further loan simultaneously from the Emperor Franz Joseph of Austria. Meanwhile he set himself the task of choosing a new Finance Minister and a new Prime Minister.

This made a tremendous impression in Munich and resulted in the strangest transactions between monarch and ministers, a bartering and bargaining which is surely unique in history and deserves to be related here in some detail.

During the following days which were full of tense excitement, an address was sent to the King signed by a small clique of citizens, of which the text was as follows:

"With the deepest devotion the undersigned humbly beg Your Majesty to resume residence, if not permanently at least regularly, in the Palace in Munich. The entire population of the capital join with us in making this request. Furthermore, as devoted subjects of Your Majesty it will be our duty and our pleasure to transfer to Your Majesty's account such a sum as shall be be sufficient to cover all outstanding debts as well as the completion of Herrenchiemsee Castle.

Respectfully awaiting Your Majesty's pleasure . . ."

The signatories to this letter were five of the most influential and best known men in the country: three industrial "kings", the owner of a great iron-foundry and a jeweller.

Unfortunately this letter, which was capable of saving the situation completely, never reached the King, for by a secret order all correspondence addressed to His Majesty passed through an "unofficial censorship" at the police-office in Munich, where this particular address was confiscated, for reasons which are very obvious.

Had the scandalous interference of this secret censorship become general knowledge, those government officials responsible for such proceedings would have been thrown out of office and the country cleansed of them for all time.

The King, henceforth realizing that he could hope for no further support from his ministers, took matters into his own hands, renewing negotiations, as a last resort, with the House of Rothschild. His attempt to raise a loan thus, was crowned with success, only to be frustrated in a dastardly manner at the last moment.

Rothschild had promised a loan of 30 or 40 million Francs at 4% interest, liable to repayment within a certain limit of time. Quartermaster Hesselschwerdt, who had also carried on the previous negotiations with Roth-schild's secretary, received the intimation that he was to proceed to Paris, taking with him the King's "I O U", when the money would be paid over to him. But at the last moment the equerry Count von Holnstein, Hessel-schwerdt's superior, intervened. On the previous occasion when Ludwig had tried to negotiate just such a loan, Holnstein had got wind of it and had said to the Quater-master threateningly:

"Obey me Hesselschwerdt, or it will cost you dear!"

It came to pass therefore, that the King's confidential messenger never reached Paris with the sealed letter con-taining the King's promissory note, but went instead to Graf Holnstein, handing him the sealed letter, remaining himself in Munich for some days in hiding. These two betrayers, Holnstein the greater and Hesselschwerdt the lesser Judas, then repaired to the Prime Minister, where-upon an audience was arranged for with Prince Luitpold, who in consequence of the incurable malady from which Prince Otto was suffering, was, as the King's uncle the next in succession.

So long as Lutz remained unmolested at the head of the Ministry there was no question of putting the King under guardianship. When however, the Catholic Party stipu-lated, at a debate in the *Landtag* on the question of co-verage for the King's debts, that they would only agree to this if he himself were put under guardianship, Lutz lost his hold of the situation completely. Even though the liberals sided with him, nothing could save him.

Shortly after this Prime Minister von Lutz discovering that the King had entrusted Baron von Franckenstein, leader of the Catholic party, with the formation of a new Cabinet, that the offer had been accepted and that von Franckenstein was preparing to proceed to Neuschwanstein Castle for an interview with Ludwig, the tragedy hanging over the King reached its ghastly climax.

To forstall the King's plans, decisions had to be made with lightning rapidity. At the same time it was necessary to conjure up some sort of legal foundation to go upon. The entire Cabinet therefore, sent an urgent demand for an audience with the King's uncle, Prince Luitpold, which was granted. In his presence the sealed letter intended for Rothschild was opened (!) and Hesselschwerdt was forbidden to carry out the King's order. Then they went to work to prove that the King was no longer responsible for his actions, producing a doctor's certificate to this effect and bringing in three other distinguished doctors in consultation, who certified the document. Immediately following this the royal family held a private consultation in Munich in the course of which they decided—with only two dissentients—to put the King under guardianship, Count von Holnstein acting as his guardian. Baron von Franckenstein was persuaded to give up his political mission, after being convinced that all was over.

The decisive document in question was the expert evidence of the famous Dr. von Gudden, Director of the General Lunatic Asylum of Upper Bavaria. It had been written and laid before the Ministry as early as the 23rd

March 1886 ready to be made use of when deemed necessary. In this fateful Cabinet-meeting it was countersigned by Dr. Hagen, Dr. Grashey, and Dr. Hubrich and was couched in the following cruel, cold-blooded terms:

> "Your Majesty is in a very advanced stage of mental disorder, a form of insanity known to brain-specialists by the name of 'Paranoia.' As this form of brain-trouble has a slow but progressive developement of many years duration, Your Majesty must be regarded as incurable, a still further decline of the mental powers being the natural developement of the disease. Suffering from such a disorder, freedom of action can no longer be allowed and Your Majesty is declared to be incapable of ruling, which incapacity will be not only for a year's duration but for the length of Your Majesty's life."

Such was the contents of the document which had lain at the disposal of the Bavarian government ever since the 23rd March 1886.

A diseased brain! Incurable!

That was not merely expert evidence, it was a sentence of death pronounced by a scientist. They wanted to prove that the great recluse-King had suddenly become a danger to his fellow-men? At last they had grasped the deadly weapon so long wished for and had turned it against him. And now the government machine had him in its ghastly clutch!

*

Sovereigns, princes and kings, Ludwig's relations, aristocrats and statesmen, discussed how to force Ludwig to abdication, the newspapers of all nations gave voice to their astonishment at the building-mania of the "fantastic" Bavarian King and the Cabinet itself in Munich made no attempt to conceal its grave anxiety at the continuance of such a form of government. Meanwhile the King, deserted by all his friends, rushed restlessly from one castle to the other, from Linderhof to Neuschwanstein, from there to Herrenchiemsee and back again to Linderhof, ostensibly inspecting the progress of building. At this time Ludwig would have gladly bartered his crown for the certainty of being able to finance all the plans he had in mind. Experience gathered in each new undertaking awakened some new idea, some new ambition. Was this restlessness really only a morbid attempt to escape from himself, as so many of Ludwig's biographers would have us believe? Was it not rather a final longing for self-expression on the part of a man who was weighed down by a sense of imminent doom?

Even his one pleasure, his self-chosen solitude was to be denied him by this bitter life, the German papers having started a campaign of critical dissection of his favourite pastimes. Meanwhile he did everything in his power to steer clear of the political intriguers and to shake himself free from his financial burdens. In the meantime his subconsciousness assumed gigantic proportions, till the one remaining interest of life, his buildings, became a mania crowding his mind's horizon and darkening the sun.

Sitting alone surrounded by fragrant flowers, in the winter-garden at Neuschwanstein the King's mind runs on this theme, thinking, thinking, planning, planning . . .

Not far away, just beyond the little town of Füssen, high up on a steep slope there stand the picturesque ruins of the fortress of Falkenstein, a landmark for the inhabitants of the Pfronten valley. It is the highest fortress in Germany, seeming to hover aloof from the world of every-day, the consort of the clouds, gazing out over a maze of mountains. Here the fourth and last of the proposed castles, the model for which stood before him in German-Gothic style, should materialize. It was to be the crowning achievement of all Ludwig's architectural ventures. (See plate 31.) Pfister, Cabinet Secretary, the successor of Düflipp, had resigned on account of this new proposal, considering it to be sheer foolishness, his place being taken by Captain Gresser. With this new secretary, who by the way had not even the remotest idea of finance, the King visited the scene of his latest project. On moonlight nights, drawn by panting horses, he would scale the rocky eminence to the ruined fortress of Frankenstein. Here, seated on the crumbling walls he would sit for hours, lost in meditation of the dim outlines of the mountain—world he so much loved.

Could he not see, or did he deliberately close his eyes to the fact that his place, at this moment of his greatest personal peril, was no longer in the mountains but in the royal Palace in Munich?

Meanwhile this man deserted of men, awaited the return of Hesselschwerdt from Paris, awaited the arrival of his newly appointed Prime Minister, Baron von Francken-stein, his weary brain planning, planning, thinking, think-ing . . .

XI. The „Arrest" of a King.

On the 5th June 1886 the Cabinet in Munich dispatched two telegrams to a certain Baron Karl Theodor Washington, who was living at the time in Poels Castle in Steiermark. The wording of the first telegram was as follows:

"You are urgently requested to travel early on Saturday to take part in consultation on important affairs. Am at home until 8.30, or from 11 o'clock onwards in the Palace. Colonel Freyschlag."

The next telegram was even more laconic:

"Am requested to demand your presence at once in consultation on a matter of business." This message bore the same signature.

Washington was a retired lieut.-colonel and held the position of chamberlain in the royal household. His connection with the King's family was of long standing, his father having married twice, his first bride being a sister of the Queen of Greece.

Prince Luitpold had hesitated long enough. He could not bring himself to make the fateful decision which would have such far-reaching results. The whole Cabinet came before him several times with urgent demands for a decision, but each time he hesitated to take the final step, always asking for more time in which to think the question over.

Sorely against his will and after an agony of mind

which few realized, he was compelled by the sheer force of circumstances to give way. The proclamation of regency however, was not to be made public until the urgent necessity for the proposed measure had been carefully and considerately laid before the King. This was Luitpold's stipulation. Consequently officials in and around Füssen were kept in the dark about the proposed change in government and even the inhabitants of Munich knew nothing definite, though they had a presentiment that something terrible was about to take place. Any rumour of the impending change which appeared in foreign newspapers was officially denied.

First thing in the morning, on Monday, the 7th June, Colonel Freyschlag received Baron von Washington with the utmost consideration, under oath of silence discussing with him state secrets of the greatest significance. The colonel then proceeded to offer him the position as the future companion to His Majesty, which offer Washington at first absolutely refused to accept. Later however, he ended by accepting the task, out of a sheer sense of duty to his unfortunate kinsman and King.

Herewith the new Commission was complete. It consisted of one of the Ministers, one *Reichsrat*, one member of the diplomatic service, one colonel and one equerry and was officially entrusted with the task of conveying a letter from the new Regent to the King. They were to be accompanied by two brain-specialists and four keepers who were instructed, after the delivery of the Regent's letter, to take the King under their care, administering medical treatment in the most "considerate" manner. The departure of these emissaries was delayed a further day, owing to a renewed access of indecision on the part of Luitpold.

At last, on the Wednesday afternoon, the Commission left Munich, via Oberdorf for Füssen. They were all oppressed by the nature of their errand and something of their depression must have transmitted itself to various railway officials, whose earnest mien showed that they suspected something very serious was on foot.

Arrived in Füssen, Baron Malsen left the group to proceed via Reutte to the Queen-Mother, to whom he was to break the news of the measures which had now become inevitable.

Towards 11 o'clock at night the Commission reached Hohenschwangau. Oppression weighed heavily upon the little group. Lights were still to be seen in the castle of Neuschwanstein opposite; the King was obviously at home, as had been duly reported in Munich. Heavy rain clouds hid the stars of the warm early-summer night.

It had been twenty-two years ago that just such a deputation had approached the castle, bringing the news to an eighteen-year-old youth of the impending death of his father, requesting him, considering the seriousness of the situation, to come down to the capital. This request had been unhesitatingly granted by a radiant youth. This same man, now unhappy and lonely, was to be condemned to eternal darkness, to life-long imprison-

ment ! Twenty-two years lay between these two occur-
rences, twenty-two fateful years.

Under trees bent with the burden of recent heavy
rains, the carriages rounded the bend to the old castle.
Here all was peaceful, only a dog's bark breaking the
stillness. The wind had dropped. From the rainbent
branches of the old maple trees bordering the drive,
drops fell like great heavy tears of portent.

There was no one to be seen at any of the windows.
None of the loyal inmates had the least idea of what
was coming, neither the grooms, nor even Weber, the
King's valet, who was the soul of loyalty. One man there
was however, who knew what was impending and what
the next few hours would bring: the butler Mayr, who
after being several times subjected to severe detailed
interrogations had been allowed to return from Munich
to the castle on the previous day. It has been said that
probably one of the castle servants called Anton Niggl
bellonged to the little circle of spies, won for the purpose. At any rate both he and Mayr were capable of
staying on until the King's departure from Neuschwanstein, ostensibly "helping" their King, though they had
long since turned against him, traitorously carrying tales
and collecting information which they placed at the disposal of the government.

Schramm, the old overseer at Hohenschwangau Castle
received the apparently harmless order to prepare rooms
in the *Kavalierbau* for members of a Baron's family. Great
was his astonishment when the gentlemen appeared. Obe-

dient, though filled with forebodings he could ill conceal, he showed them to their respective rooms, after being convinced by them that their came in the name of the government. Down in the entrance-hall four more men in black suits were waiting.

„Are you in attendance on the gentlemen upstairs?"

"No, we are keepers from the asylum, brought by Dr. Gudden."

Schramm could hardly believe his ears, especially when he heard one of the men ask his companion:

"Have you got white gloves for us to wear when we go into the King's room?"

What was the meaning of all this?

The old man, in a state of the utmost agitation, went off into the background, where he rang up Mayr, the butler at Neuschwanstein.

"Is everything in order over there?"

"Absolutely. Why?"

"All your lights have gone out suddenly, which is most unusual."

"The King hasn't been able to sleep for several days and was so exhausted that he dozed off sitting reading in bed; he's sleeping quietly now, like everyone else."

"Well, but doesn't he know that he has to grant an audience on some important business soon?"

"Yes——"

"Well, when shall I send the gentlemen over, at four o'clock?"

"Good gracious no ! That's much too late; he will have gone out by then. At three, as arrang—— !"

"What ?"

"Nothing ! At three !"

While this was going on the gentlemen at Hohenschwangau Castle held a last conference in strict privacy. They went once more over all the points to be remembered, the manner in which the "insane" man was to receive the Regent's proclamation and the most harmless way to parry the questions he would be sure to ask. The chief doctor disputed excitedly with the *Reichsrat*, Count Törring, the latter stipulating that anything inconsiderate either in word or deed must be avoided, seeing that after all they were dealing with a King. The arrangement decided on at last, was as follows: Baron von Crailsheim, as Minister of State and President of the Commission was to go first, the two guardians, Count Törring and Count von Holnstein, supporting him one on each side. Then the two doctors, accompanied by *Legationsrat* Rumpler, whose instructions were to take a complete report of the proceedings, should enter, whilst the four keepers were to wait outside the door in case of a sudden fit of frenzy on the part of His Majesty. They were instructed in such an event to overpower the King. But they could not agree on the question of whether, on account of the unusual height and strength of the sick man, a strait-waistcoat would be necessary or not.

On Count von Holnstein's refusing, out of respect for royal prestige, to agree to the King driving to Linderhof alone in the carriage with two of the keepers, as Dr. Gudden wished, suggesting that it would be enough if the new adjutant, Baron von Washington, were to accompany him, the doctor averred testily that even a King, once declared to be insane, was under doctor's orders. So after a tremendous amount of discussion it was decided to let the King drive to Linderhof alone, with only one of the keepers on the box by the coachman, the doctors following in the next carriage. Furthermore Gudden required the door of the King's carriage to be secured on the outside with a strap making it impossible to open it from the inside, telling stories of his experience with lunatics and of sudden attempts at escape.

To procure the necessary strap for the King's carriage door-handle, they had to wake the castle saddler. This produced a tremendous and quite unexpected sensation amongst the servants, who assembled excitedly discussing they knew not what. Then these simple people fetched their farmer-friends from the village to stand by and help them, talking of robbery, of an attempt on the King's life, of kidnapping and of indescribable torture.

The "High" Commission however, did not let all this excitement worry them in the least. They even found time to repair to the village inn, Hotel Lisl, in Hohenschwangau and there to sit down to a seven-course (!) dinner washed down with ten bottles of champagne and forty quarts of beer. The menu bore the title *"Souper de la Majesté le roi"*. Of such coarseness were these men capable, whose services were remunerated by the state ! On the back of this menu—which has now become a historical document—there was a rough sketch of the particular room in Linderhof where the King was to be kept.

Under the influence of considerable quantities of alcohol, Count von Holnstein very nearly upset his Commission's carefully laid plans, by being all too clever. Stepping out of the little inn, into the street he saw Osterholzer, the King's coachman, harnessing the horses to Ludwig's carriage. As usual His Majesty intended to go driving at 3 a. m. Thereupon the Count ordered the horses unharnessed again, making some unwise remark about another carriage being used driven by another coachman.

"But these were the King's orders !"

"The King will give no more orders: you will take orders in future only from His Royal Highness Prince Luitpold. Do you understand ?"

The Count had gone too far. Here was he, daring to make such remarks, and Ludwig himself had not the remotest suspicion of the abdication which was to be forced upon him. The Count's bravado was destined to be short-lived however, for not long after this he was trembling for his life like a hunted animal. That he escaped scot-free was no credit to himself, but to the King's servants.

In any case this remark of Count Holnstein, had opened the coachman's eyes completely. He led his horses back to the stables and then slipped out into the night, hurrying as fast as his legs would carry him, stumbling in the darkness along a steep little private path through the forest, over to Neuschwanstein Castle. He found the castle servant Niggl dozing on a bench, whom he sent flying off to findWeber the valet telling him to waken the King at once.

Osterholzer entered the King's room a few minutes later, throwing himself on his knees before him. But in his breathlesness and excitement he could only stammer a few disconnected words, which were unintelligible. The King turned to Weber for an explanation, who told him that down in the valley there were people who had hostile intentions of some sort against his person.

The King, visibly unnerved, spoke to his valets as man to man, instead of only through the door, as had been usual up till now. They answered him aloud too, forgetting that they had been strictly forbidden to do more than to move their hand in dumb sign of assent. Osterholzer advised immediate flight and Weber promised his help, come what might. But the King refused all offers of help saying:

"Why should I fly? If there were really any danger, Karl would have sent me word from Munich."

This Karl was Hesselschwerdt, one of his treacherous "friends", but in whom he still, without the least misgivings, had the greatest confidence.

After a few moments reflection Ludwig assembled the whole staff together and ordered them to gather all the loyal peasants of the neighbourhood at the castle and to alarm the Schwangau fire-brigade. This was towards 2 o'clock at night.

All around an impenetrable mist clung to the mountain peaks. From the west these phantom cloud-forms gathered, gradually filling in the contours of the mountains, as if to hide something from the world, something scandalous and irrevocable. Here too, 3000 ft. up, the three days continuous rain had left larches and pines heavy with moisture.

At Neuschwanstein, the windows of the great building were once more full of lights. Not only in the castle itself, but down in the valley there were signs of unusual animation. The arrival of a deputation from the capital had become known and these gentlemen, who had just hurried into their uniforms were left in no doubt that, owing to Count Holnstein's indiscretion, their position was a very disagreeable one. A shudder passed over each one of them as after only a short rest the little group set out towards Neuschwanstein, which now loomed tremendous through the mist, a glowing phantom.

The Commission approached the great edifice by the broad road which zig-zagged steeply up from the village. They were actually daring to undertake to tell him, who was one of the first intercedents for the founding of a German Empire, the great devotee of Richard Wagner and pioneer on behalf of his art, the greatest romanticist amongst kings, that he was to be deposed and put into the charge of asylum-doctors. It were better had they been struck dumb than to presume to put such a man as Ludwig under guardianship, a man who not only bodily but also intellectually, was head and shoulders above them all. Yet specialists dared to declare a man to be insane who was merely eccentric without even an examination, who se opinions on most subjects were far more normal than those of the majority of the supercultivated intellectuals!

Deplore it as one may——the irrevocable deed was to be accomplished.

In the meantime 3 o'clock had struck.

At the entrance to the castle, eight policemen on foot and two mounted police took up their positions with loaded rifles and fixed bayonets. The "mad" King had quickly found the means to overthrow even the most carefully laid plans of the Commission.

In less than one hour the stable boys and servants had alarmed all the neighbouring villages. In less than one hour, from Hohenschwangau to Füssen, and beyond, as far as Schwangau, the country-side swarmed with loyal, faithful peasants, who when they heard that an attack on their King was planned assembled, armed with knives, ready to risk their lives for him. Füssen had even sent their whole fire-brigade, headed by the police-inspector who was stationed there.

At the entrance to the castle, the Commission was refused admittance. Their spokesman, Count von Holnstein, thereupon explained that the Commission came on behalf of Prince Luitpold, to present the King with an official document, showing as he spoke the signature of His Royal Highness. This was an explanation that the Count, generally so cool and reserved, should not have needed to make after having got as far as the entrance to the castle. The sergeant-major, hardly glancing at the papers, replied:

"I need no papers! I obey only *one* order and that is His Majesty's. I am the father of a family, but you can have me shot for this, for all I care. All I know is that I have His Majesty's orders to carry out. I refuse to admit you and am, if necessary, ready to use force to prevent your entrance."

However painful this whole affair was, at any rate none of the members of the Commission could deny that these sentinels did their duty faithfully. All the smart uniforms failed to make any impression on them: they stuck to their original statement that they had "His Majesty's orders to carry out".

Hardly had the sergeant-major finished speaking than a woman approached the entrance and shouted:

"I won't give him up; he is mine! I'll never give him over to traitors!"

It was the Russian Baroness, Spera von Truchsess, who in consequence of ill-health often came to the neigh-bouring health-resort, Kaufbeuren, for treatment. She had cherished a secret adoration for Ludwig for a long time and in order to be near him had built herself a small castle on the main road between Füssen and Schwangau. Dr. von Gudden recognized the excited lady immediately as a former patient of his and said somewhat sarcastically to his assistant:

"This fool of a woman is the last straw." The Baroness

meanwhile, who seemed to know most of the members of the Commission, continued to make caustic remarks to the little group.

She managed to accomplish however, what others could not. Beating wildly about with her umbrella she eluded the rough grasp of the keepers and police, somehow reaching the King's room. Here she repeated over and over again that she was ready to defend her beloved Ludwig to the last drop of her blood, reporting word for word all that had passed at the castle-entrance, volubly urging the King to lose no time in setting out for Munich.

The King, shaking hands with her on the threshold of his room answered patiently:

"Don't you think you had better send for your husband to accompany you back to your villa?"

But the Baroness pretended not to hear and continued with the utmost vehemence to argue with Ludwig, ending by placing at his disposal her whole fortune. The King cooly waived away the Russian millions, which would have been more than enough to cover all his debts, not because he was not in his right mind, but because at this moment of pressing personal danger, his German pride would not allow him to accept her offer. At last, worn out he rang for his valet, telling him to show the Baroness to another room, as her excitable conversation "bored" him.

In the meantime the members of the Commission made an attempt to force an entrance. This only had the effect of making the sentries raise their rifles, whilst the rest of the police advanced, injuring one of the keepers with a blow from the butt-end of a rifle. Simultaneously a little bottle fell to the ground, the contents of which smelt strongly of chloroform. The sergeant-major shouted:

"For the last time, in the name of His Majesty I warn you: one step more and I fire!"

"Very well, we will return to Hohenschwangau Castle and from Munich you will receive further orders",

was the somewhat faint-hearted reply of Count von Holnstein.

And this was actually what happened. The Commission retraced their steps to the old castle, their mission unfulfilled. What a retreat it was, too! From the valleys and ravines of all that mountainous district, the fire-brigade men were hurrying towards the castle. Some of them, from the more distant farms, had been brought at a gallop by farmer Niggl in his farm-cart as far as Hohenschwangau Castle. Determination was imprinted on every face and all were armed to the teeth. Carrying storm-lanterns they gathered from far and near, the swaying lights twinkling in the darkness, all converging in the one direction as if bent on some deadly deed. It was lucky for the gentlemen of the Commission that for the time at least they were neither recognized nor molested.

The rumour that the King was to be kidnapped had spread like wild-fire through the whole district of Schwanengau. Down in the village of Hohenschwangau the little high—street was a surging mass of shouting young fellows from all the farms around, armed with flails, choppers, axes, hay-forks and the long Bavarian knives. They were augmented by the game-keepers, wood-cutters and masons, all ready to defend their King. The great gentlemen from Munich had their work cut out to push through the moving masses of men streaming uphill towards the castle. With all the speed at their command they beat a retreat to the old castle of Hohenschwangau, where at least they anticipated shelter.

This time, when it was a question of their own safety, they lost no time in discussions, deciding unanimously (!) to get new orders from Munich, and to come back later to take possession of the King by force. But Ludwig's fury knew no bounds. He made arrangements to render any decision that they came to of no avail. The "despicable traitors" should be made to suffer and the "scoundrelly pack" should have a frightful sentence served on them for their criminal insubordination!

All his life Ludwig had despised nothing so much as unfaithfulness and betrayal, he who had had enough experience of such things in his lonely life. His state of mind now was nothing short of black fury: was he King or was he it no longer?

It was in the early hours of the morning that police-inspector Boppeler was sent for by the King and given the order to arrest all the members of the Commission.

These gentlemen were in the act of undressing, when they were surprised and led away. Minister Crailsheim openly attacked Boppeler, maintaining that he had no

Bild 31: Burgmodell zum Falkenstein
Model of Falkenstein Castle

Bild 32: Todesstelle im See mit Denkmal

Memorial Cross in the lake at the spot where the drowned King was found

right to act as he was doing, to which that worthy man answered quite simply:

"Your Excellency! I am in a very painful situation. We were not in the least prepared for this occurrence. We have had no orders at all as to what our duty might be on such an occasion. But I've served His Majesty very many years and am still in his service. All in a few moments I can neither forget the love and devotion of a life-time, nor can I behave as a traitor to my King."

They were all arrested except *Legationsrat* Rumpler. It was characteristic that he managed to escape observation. He had been seen standing below near the stables in his red uniform and had not been taken for one of the important delegates from Munich, but for a member of an acrobatic troupe that happened at the time to be in Hohenschwangau.

The manner of their return to Neuschwanstein was even more undignified than their retreat had been. Count Holnstein insisted that they should be driven, but the police-inspector had no sympathy with his sensitive feelings on this subject. All of the gentlemen were compelled to go on foot through the excited mob of villagers. The zig-zag road up to the castle was swarming with people gathered from far and near, ready to bash the brains out of any opponent. It needed considerable efforts on the part of the fire-men and police to prevent the infuriated mob from putting their threats into practice.

For a time the person most in danger seemed to be Dr. von Gudden, for the people had in the meantime heard that it was at his instigation that the King was to be declared insane. On reaching the castle courtyard several men rushed at him, swearing they would throw the "dirty scoundrel" into the roaring torrent of the Pöllat river, near by.

None of the villagers assembled knew anything about Minister Feilitzsch's proclamation in Munich, as this had been kept secret from the officials in Schwangau until the King himself should have been informed of the wording of the proclamation. But was that really the only reason? The Palace had not shown such touching consideration on other occasions, for were they not capable of declaring a man to be insane without even having him medically examined? Was not the cause of this secretiveness their fear of the King's many staunch adherents? Probably those at the Palace had not such clear consciences as many would have us believe.

One word from the King would have been enough for his faithful German peasant-folk to rally to his call in full strength, ready to help their beloved King to defend the throne of which he was to be robbed, faithful to the last drop of their blood. Here in the darkness they stood their ground in threatening groups like great innocent children defending their rights. They thirsted to destroy these "lascivious town-fellows", these "scoundrels in their glaring uniforms"! They only waited the word of command from the King.

When the prisoners had been temporarily locked into a little room belonging to one of the wood-cutters, the air vibrated with the triumphant cries of "Long live the King". It was not until later on, when the district-magistrate from Füssen arrived, who took over the superintendence of affairs that the order was given to transfer the prisoners to other rooms, guarded by four policemen. Feeling had risen to fever-heat when in the carriages belonging to the Commission not only narcotics, but straps and even strait-waistcoats had been found, leaving no further doubt as to the methods to be employed in overpowering the King.

The position of the prisoners became increasingly critical and no one could tell what was in store for them. Crailsheim scribbled hastily on a scrap of paper:

"Send help at once: we are in great danger. The King has ordered us to be put to death."

A man-servant was bribed to smuggle this message over to Hohenschwangau Castle to *Legationsrat* Rumpler.

Meanwhile the King, in great agitation paced his rooms above in a state of blind fury, the outcome of many months of bitter deceptions. But on hearing from his valet Weber, that his life-long friend Count Holnstein was amongst the delegates, he was beside himself and forgetting all bounds he cried:

"The prisoners are to be chained and then lashed with the whip. Food and drink are to be withheld and later, their eyes are to be put out."

In his access of sudden fury Ludwig wrote this order to be put into immediate execution. To understand this one must remember that he was the victim of the most despicable, carefully planned deception and of treachery of the lowest order.

Crailsheim, on hearing of the fate to be meted out to the members of the Commission, offered a high sum of money to ransom his own person. Holnstein at least possessed more courage, begging one of the guards to shoot him to save him from worse dishonour. The district magistrate, who had meanwhile successfully quietened the mob outside, persuading them to disperse, was undecided what steps to take next and the guards themselves were reluctant to carry out the King's order.

At last, after two hours of anxious waiting, a decision was come to. The Prince Regent's proclamation was telegraphed to the district-magistrate at Füssen. He immediately released the members of the Commission, read the telegraphed information to the fire-men and police, allowing the gentlemen from Munich to leave the castle one by one, unobserved. After the receipt of a second telegram the magistrate himself retired from further participation in the events, on the score of allegiance to the new government. With much difficulty, making a wide detour of the neighbouring villages, the Commission reached the Palace in Munich by round-about ways without being molested, where they presented their report to Prime Minister Lutz.——

*

All the details of the carefully planned attack on his person Ludwig had brought to naught by clear, logical action betraying no trace of insanity. With just the same clarity of perception he had telegraphed during that terrible night for his personal aide-de-camp, Count Alfred von Dürckheim-Montmartin, to come to him. He had realized that he could no longer depend on the members of his own household and that many of them must be spies and traitors. In any case he had come to the conclusion that it might prove his undoing not to have a single friend to stand by him when it came to a question of personal danger. In such moments he had learnt to put complete confidence in Dürckheim, who since May 1883 had served him with the utmost devotion.

Restlessly the unhappy man paced to and fro in his great throne-room, his mind tortured with a thousand doubts. Sometimes he stood gazing out with great melancholy eyes upon the vast panorama of mountains—his wonder-land—his thoughts reverting to many a day of unclouded happiness spent in these solitudes he so much loved, days of sheer sublimity far from the petty worries that assailed most men. Will Dürckheim come, or is he too a traitor, just another of those scoundrels whom Ludwig imagined still under arrest below?

Dürckheim came——and sooner than Ludwig had dared to hope for. On his father's estate where he had been staying, sensational rumours had reached him, which had given him food for anxiety. On a sweating, exhausted horse he arrived at Hohenschwangau, changing rapidly at Hotel Alpenrose into his uniform, and now stood before his master, his King, as Ludwig's sole remaining friend. At the entrance to the castle he had dismissed the members of the fire-brigade with a few appreciative words.

The sight of Ludwig in a state of complete collapse was a terrible shock to him. The King was sitting on the edge of his bed still talking to himself about rascally scoundrels and despicable beasts. At a slight sound he suddenly sprang up shouting:

"Such ministers ought to be put in a cage and exhibited all over Germany; at every fair, on every occasion, such wretches should be shown up for what they are: the scum of the earth!"

Dürckheim tried to soothe him:

"Your Majesty must try not to forget his usual prudence and presence of mind in moments like these when his person is in danger."

"What do you mean by that? Are you trying to break some more bad news to me? Speak out! I, the King, am ready for everything."

"Well——somehow I don't like the attitude of the officials at Füssen."——

"How do you mean? Don't keep me in suspense. Is it some new deception?"

"If I am not mistaken, the district-magistrate sent a telegram to Munich asking for information!"

"Why? What could induce him to do so and how did you get to know it?"

"One of the postmen told me in strict confidence."

"But what did the magistrate ask about?"

"I dare not put it into words before Your Majesty!"

"But I insist upon your doing so !"

"He asked, whether Your Majesty's uncle had really taken over the Regency————"

"*The Re———gen———cy* ?"

Ludwig's voice seemed like the echo of a cry. He went deadly pale and Dürckheim was silent.

"So it's got as far as that already, has it ! A Regency ! Behind my back the Palace has managed to unseat me after all."

"I'm afraid so, Your Majesty."

The King sank back into his chair, remaining a few moments as if turned to stone. Dürckheim almost held his breath.

"If the Füssen magistrate really put that question ————if the reply was really in the affirmative———— if————"

Dürckheim remained silent, hardly daring to even look up. The King now knew exactly how things stood. Tears welled up in Ludwig's eyes. A sudden agony of shivering took possession of his whole frame and great sobs shook him with an almost child-like abandon. For now the immensity of what had happened dawned upon him. His own helplessness, in all its vastness and terror made chaos in his mind; he felt himself being crushed and swept off his feet in an avalanche of hideousness. The death-stroke had been dealt.

Patiently Dürckheim argued with the King that his best plan was to parry the blow; that he should go to the capital and appear before his loyal people with all the confidence of king-ship, thus scattering to the four winds of heaven the dastardly assertion that he was insane.

There is no doubt that this sensible advice, had it been carried out, would have proved to be the best and indeed the only means of setting Ludwig free again. The Bavarians would have rallied to their King, loyal to a man. Ludwig himself however, could not be persuaded to believe this, probably because too much had happened at once which had undermined his confidence and had taken him completely unawares. He replied that at present he was altogether too exhausted, but that he would go to Munich the next day. Half-asleep, in a state of utter exhaustion, with a touch of appeal in his voice he said:

"Send somebody reliable to Bismarck!"

Although the new government had omitted to advise the officials of the Schwangau district of the coming change, they had taken the precaution of warning all the post-offices in the neighbourhood. This meant that in future none of Ludwig's telegrams could be despatched from a Bavarian telegraph-office, but had to be handed in across the frontier in Tyrol. Dürckheim therefore, set out personally to ride to Reutte in Tyrol with the proposed telegram to Bismarck, to ensure the message being safely sent.

Bismarck's reply gave the same advice as Dürckheim had given, whereupon the King declared his definite intention of travelling to the capital the following day. The adjutant thereupon drew up a proclamation to the Bavarian people and the whole German nation, affixed the date of the previous day to it laying it before Ludwig for his signature. It read as follows:

"Prince Luitpold, against my will, intends to declare himself Prince Regent of my country. My former Cabinet by untruthful assertions regarding my state of health has deceived my beloved people and has been guilty of preparing an act of high-treason. I am in mind and body as healthy as any other monarch, but the proposed act of high-treason has come into being so unexpectedly that no time remains to me to frustrate the criminal intentions of the Cabinet by countervailing measures. In the case therefore, of the above mentioned illegal measures being carried out and Prince Luitpold, against my will declaring himself Prince Regent, I hereby charge my loyal subjects, by every means in their power to defend my rights.

From all dutiful Bavarian officials, especially from honourable Bavarian officers and every brave Bavarian soldier I expect loyalty. Mindful of their oath of allegiance to me I expect them to remain true to me and faithfully to serve me in this dark hour and to take up arms for me against the traitors within our walls. Every royalist Bavarian is hereby summoned to resist Prince Luitpold and the former Cabinet as being guilty of high-treason. I know that I and my beloved people stand united and I am firmly convinced that my subjects will rally to my call, to defend me against the proposed act of high-treason.

Given under my hand and seal at Hohenschwangau
on the 9th June 1886.

Ludwig,

King of Bavaria, Count Palatine etc."

Unfortunately this proclamation could now no longer
be communicated to the country by means of Bavarian
telegraph-offices, but had to be distributed in the form
of a leaflet. Meanwhile Dürckheim, the solitary man's last
remaining friend, continued to work feverishly. He wrote
a long telegram to the Emperor of Austria, asking for
his intervention to prevent the outbreak of a bloody civil-
war and to the prospective Prime Minister, Baron von
Franckenstein, he sent an express-message requesting him
to form a new Cabinet without delay. Dürckheim shouted
to the mounted messenger as he rode off:

"To Reutte as fast as ever you can, even if four
horses are ridden to death!"

The Empress Elisabeth of Austria, who happened to
be staying at her summer residence on Starnberg lake,
used all her influence to try to persuade her husband to
intervene.

The last and the most important of all these telegrams
and the one which promised to be of the most practical
use, passed unfortunately through the hands of the butler,
Mayr, the traitor. It was a summons to General Muck of
the Kempten Rifle-battalion to come immediately to Neuschwanstein Castle to the defence of His Majesty's person.
Mayr, cunning fellow that he was, saw fit to add a few
words to the text of the telegram which suggested to

the General the advisability of first securing the permission of the War-Ministry. The War-Ministry refused, the rifle-battalion received no orders to proceed to Neuschwanstein: King and adjutant waited in vain, knowing nothing of the butler's interference.

It was with a heavy heart that Dürckheim stood once more before the King:

"Have my orders regarding the members of the Commission been carried out?"

"Your Majesty——"

"Have they been carried out, yes or no?"

"Your Majesty——the Füssen magistrate got a reply-telegram————the gentlemen had to be released——"

"You traitor!"

"Your Majesty——I must take that hard word upon me although I could not have prevented the release ——the prisoners were gone before I arrived!"

The King laughed grimly.

"Am I still King in my own country, or not?"

"Your Majesty——I don't know!"

"Ha! ha! ha! Oh, the traitors! the miserable traitors!"

Desperate, despairing, Ludwig paced up and down, alternately clenching his fists and gesticulating wildly; not until the access of fury had spent itself, did he sink down in a state of utter collapse.

Another two hours passed slowly. The Kempten Rifles had still not come and the King lost the last traces of that will to resist, to which he had nerved himself. He declared point blank his inability to travel to Munich without the support of the troops, adding that in his present state of nerve-strain and looking so ill as he did, he could not bring himself to appear in public.

Dürckheim was seized with despair. It became clear to him that there was no chance of saving his beloved King, for whom inexpressible misery was in store. He gathered all his powers of persuasion together, urging Ludwig to immediate flight:

"Delay is fatal: Your Majesty is in extreme danger! Escape over the frontier: seek the protection of the Emperor of Austria and his noble wife. It is only a matter of a few hours from here. I do urgently beg Your Majesty to take this chance before it is too late, and I will answer for it with my life! Follow me on horseback through the back-gateway of the castle, along the huntsman's path, over the pass beyond Ammerwald; or of you will not do that, at least leave here for Linderhof Castle."

Twice while Dürckheim spoke he saw a flicker of interest pass over Ludwig's face: once when he mentioned the Empress of Austria and the second time at the word Linderhof. The light of interest however, quickly died out of his eyes.

"Escape? I, the King, am to fly before these scoundrels? *Never*! I'll never give in to them: the troops must soon be here and then I'll defend myself. My castle is impregnable: let them dare to besiege me and I'll pay them out, every one of the damned scoundrels !"

A sudden knock on the door made Ludwig start.

"They've come, Dürckheim ! They've got me this time. Everyone is against me !"

Mayr entered with a telegram for Dürckheim. It was from the Ministry of War, ordering Dürckheim to report at once in Munich.

"Your Majesty, what shall I do now ? If I remain here I am guilty of insubordination. Only a royal command can annul such an order. Does Your Majesty feel able to do this ?"

"I won't offer any more opposition. Write to my uncle requesting him to let you remain with me."

Ludwig, with these words virtually acknowledged the power of the "rebels". He made one despairing effort to retain the last of his friends, but even this was to be denied him soon, for the Prince Regent's answer read as follows:

"The order rests with the Ministry of War."

*

Meanwhile, the rain still fell incessantly.

Dürckheim, who had been called in too late to be of any real help, had gone; Ludwig was more solitary than ever.

The lonely man wandered from room to room like a lost child, and whilst from every dark corner horror seemed to stare out at him, the ghastly deed of treachery was completed. Act after act, scene after scene of the carefully arranged programme was enacted, in secret.

In his castle, the King awaited the arrival of 300 loyal soldiers from Kempten. Had they also, with one accord, all turned traitors ?

And *still* Ludwig waited ! but they never came. In their stead appeared suddenly at the bend of the zig-zag road, bright uniforms and the glint of arms. They were forty-eight newly sworn-in government police from Munich, who took up their position on the crest of the hill, occupied the castle and closed the road to Austria. The King thought they had come to protect him, whereas from that moment onwards he was an unwitting prisoner. No longer inviolate, the Castle of the Holy Grail had been desecrated !

It was not until he was refused his usual midnight drive, that the whole horror of his position was borne in upon him. Then at last he realized that in his own castle, in his own land, he was a helpless prisoner.

Death-like silence descended upon the castle: only in the royal rooms the restless man paced to and fro ceaselessly. In vain he awaited Dürckheim's return from Munich. All contact with the outside world seemed completely cut off, yet Ludwig still found it difficult to believe that ingratitude is the world's wage !

XII. The King under Guardianship.

On the 10th June, the government issued a proclamation to the effect that the King's uncle had taken over the administration of the country and that the *Landtag* would assemble.

Towards 11 o'clock a.m. a Cabinet council was held in the Palace. It was decided that two brain-specialists, together with 4 keepers, should take charge of His Majesty and that he should be taken direct to Berg Castle and not, as at first proposed, to Linderhof, for fear of his escaping over the Tyrolese frontier.

From now onwards, anyone who still hoped to set the King free, risked being considered guilty of high-treason against the new government. The inhabitants of Hohenschwangau however, troubled their heads little about the risks they ran. Beyond the frontier 150 men stood ready to wrest the King from his persecutors. They all reckoned on Ludwig's escape by the huntsman's path through the forest over to Tyrol and from thence by carriage to Vienna to the Emperor.——

Ludwig's agitation of the previous day had given place to a composure almost amounting to indifference. Did he after all intend to submit to his terrible fate without the least resistance?

The fact that the whole country round was once more shrouded in thick fog, making everything 10 paces ahead indistinguishable and that the new police were complete strangers to the district, induced a number of courageous villagers to attempt to rescue the prisoner. To this end it was necessary first to win over the butler Mayr. He however, had no intention of being drawn into any such attempt and never even told Ludwig that people were trying to help him. It seems however, that Weber, the King's valet, must have informed his master that something was on foot, but not until it was too late, for Ludwig asked whether such an attempt to rescue him could be effected without loss of life. On hearing that no one could guarantee this, he tried to dismiss the idea from his mind. But the suggestion having once been made, took hold of his imagination and he began to plan an escape on his own account, accompanied by his coachman, Osterholzer. He therefore sent for Osterholzer, only to learn that, as a precautionary measure, the coachman had been removed from the castle on account of his well-know royalist leanings.

On being informed shortly after this of the latest proposals to put him under the guardianship of brain-specialists and keepers, one idea occupied Ludwig's mind to the exclusion of all else, and that was the desire to commit suicide. Up and down the great throne-room he paced with heavy tread. Presently he rang for Weber, telling him to remain in the room with him. Sometimes he would read, sometimes would stand glaring into space. Once he asked the valet whether he believed in the immortality of the soul and the punishment of sin, for, said Ludwig

Bild 33: Das Todeszimmer in Schloß Berg

Bild 34: König Ludwig II. schlägt einen Georgiritter

Nach einem Aquarell von F. Eibner King Ludwig II. conferring the Knighthood of St. George
König Ludwig II. Museum in Herrenchiemsee

"what they propose to do to me will most certainly bring its own punishment".

"That they have deprived me of my throne, I could perhaps become accustomed to, but that they call me insane will kill me. *My blood be upon those who have betrayed me and who seek my destruction*! To be plunged from the heights into such a living death as this, is more than I can stand. Life is over for me. To be treated like my brother Otto, at the mercy of any keeper who likes to bully him, who even threatenes him with blows if he doesn't obey, would be more than I could endure."

He tourned as he finished speaking, towards his study, ordering Weber to accompany him. There he collected from the drawers of his writing-table all the money he happened to have. It amounted to 1200 Marks, which he handed to his faithful servant, his eyes brimming with tears. Then he caught up his hat, loosening from it the diamond buckle, saying:

"Take my diamond buckle too and this promissory note as well. Should they force you to give up the diamonds, this document will at any rate compensate you to the amount of 25,000 Marks."

His Prayer-book, worn with much use, he also gave to Weber, with the words: "Pray for me!"

The thought of death had taken a mighty hold upon him now. He went out onto the balcony once more, and with head in hands sat there staring out into the night. Sleep had utterly forsaken him. Was he still waiting for the 300 soldiers from Kempten?

Suddenly, assailed by an access of terror, he stepped back into the room, ordering Weber sharply to go and get him some cyanide of potassium.

"I must be prepared. They shan't take me alive. Nothing will induce me to submit to being caged up. To give myself over to the mercy of these miserable persecutors, is more than my pride allows."

But one servant after the other refused to procure the poison for him. He then demanded from Mayr the key to the great tower.

"When my hair-dresser comes in the morning, tell him to search the river Pöllat for my head. I pray for God's mercy and forgiveness. The pain that this will give my Mother, I would gladly spare her, but death is forced upon me."

Mayr meanwhile secretly telegraphed to Munich: "fear attempt at suicide. Poison has been demanded."

From the battlements of the highest tower the unhappy man intended to plunge to a ghastly death. The cunning butler however, had enough presence of mind to withhold from his master the desired key for some considerable time, maintaining that he had mislaid it.

Like a ghost, like a mere shadow of his former self Ludwig paced to and fro, up and down, all through that endless night of horror. The great mirrors in his rooms, reflected a sorry sight: his black hair, through which he repeatedly ran his nervous fingers, hung limp and dishevelled over his brow. His great eyes, admirable even in his present despair, glowed with an unearthly radiance.

"Won't my people raise a finger to help their King ?"
he cried despairingly.

"Your Majesty, the people have no weapons", answered
the valet.

The strain of the long delay began to tell upon him.
With uncertain step he reached the great dining-hall. Feeling the need of a stimulant, he ordered wine, brandy and
cigarettes. He, who had never been a drinker, now resorted
to alcohol, seeking forgetfulness and finding none. At any
price, even at the price of his life, he was determined to
escape the clutches of that man, who with cold scientific
calculation was preparing to plunge him into outer-dark-
ness, into oblivion. Would this man, with his four hellp-
ers, really dare to return, to drag their victim to execution ?

*

New delegates had been chosen: Dr. von Gudden,
Director of the Lunatic-Asylum, with Dr. Müller as his
assistant, eight keepers and the chief of the Munich police-
force. As soon as the Prince Regent's proclamation had
been made public in Hohenschwangau, these gentlemen
were to appear before the imprisoned King. Mayr, the
butler, was requisitioned to give the sign when he considered the moment propitious for seizing the King.

Once more the lonely man stood on his balcony, his
gaze wandering from one beloved landmark to another.
Around him rose and fell the peaceful mountain-peaks;
opposite, shrouded in the mists of morning, stood his

father's castle. There is was, as a youth, that he had aspired to a noble task, that of creating a realm given over to the cult of beauty. And what thanks had he received? Unhurriedly, peacefully the great master-musician, Wagner, had passed over into immortality, whilst he, the King, in what despair must he bid farewell to his "dream-castle" Neuschwanstein, his enchanted Herrenchiemsee, his magical Linderhof and in what dishonour must he forsake the gentian-spangled slopes and the sapphire waters of the Alpsee!

That the whole country round still hung heavy with rain-clouds was in some ways a good thing, for in rain a parting is easier to bear than in sparkling sunshine. On a gloomy day it seemed less hard to cast crown and purple down, nor was it even so difficult to cast one's very life away, when the sun was veiled. When these traitorous fellows, with their paid helpers, forced their way in, they should find the great rooms deserted, save for the corpse of their victim.

With these and other thoughts of a like nature, Ludwig's mind busied itself hour after hour. In nervous agitation he had paced from room to room, till all at once his mood changed. He rang the bell with sudden decision. Mayr, that despicable hypocrite, entered.

"Bring more wine and brandy and some iced champagne as well. Do you understand? Let us be cheerful, my good fellow. Let's drown our sorrows and make the farewell easier to bear. From the castle of the Holy Grail no one shall drag me, like a helpless animal. Half an hour after midnight I was born: at the self-same hour I will die !"

Mayr left the room, returning a little later with the champagne.

"Is it well mixed, my lad ? Enough poison to work quickly, to spare me the ghastly plunge from the tower ?"

"*Your Majesty* !"

"Ha ! ha ! 'Majesty' ! That's good ! That's all over now and you know it. Here's to myself !"

Eagerly, hastily, Ludwig drained off three or four glasses in quick succession.

"And where's that key, my lad. If you don't hand it over at once, I'll strangle you——you remember, I nearly did that once before ? This is my last royal command——:hand over the key to the tower !"

To himself he laughed hollowly. A "royal command" indeed ! That sounded well from a man who was no longer a King but just a lunatic ! Mayr stood rooted to the spot, not knowing what to do. For a whole year he had not been allowed to communicate with the King aloud, only by means of signs. Not one sentence had been exchanged until lately, yet for the past two days the King had talked to him like a friend.

"The key to the tower——the key to the tower !" Ludwig kept on repeating and ground his teeth in such a manner that Mayr made a sudden dash for liberty.

*

The new delegation, who have gone down to history under the name of the "Arrest-commission", had now arrived for the second time in Neuschwanstein Castle, headed by the director of the lunatic-asylum. This time the new sentinels let them pass without demur. As arranged, the butler Mayr was at once sent for. He gave his report, telling with feigned anxiety the King's desire for the key to the tower, asking Dr. von Gudden helplessly what he should do about it. He added that he had the key in his pocket, but that he felt he could not possibly hand it over to the King.

This episode inspired the experienced asylum-director with the bright idea of coming upon the King unawares, just inside the door of the tower. Ludwig should then be told that his brain was disordered and that what he was on the point of doing was an act of insanity. If necessary he was to be forcibly overpowered. The police-officier, Horn, was to act as witness and was commissioned to give the order for force to be used. Strange that it should be a police-officer to whom this duty fell, but then after all, what was a mere king?

Through half-finished corridors, along loose boarding, they all hurried to the spiral-staircase of the tower. The scene was set!

Within the great room, someone's ears caught unaccustomed sounds. What was that? Footsteps of strange men? What were they doing in the marble-corridors of his castle?

The champagne bottle was half empty. Ludwig drained

the last drops into his glass. His hand trembled, his cigarette fell to the floor unheeded. Who was that speaking? The sounds reached him quite plainly; there could be no mistake about it. What did all this mean?

A presentiment that something frightful was about to take place, threatened to overpower his senses, though he still fought against the feeling. Suddenly, the tortures of persecution-mania descended upon him. He rushed to the window, wrestling wildly with the lock, intending from the balcony of his beloved castle to plunge... At this moment Mayr entered:

"Your Majesty! Your Majesty! The key to the tower has been found!"

The King murmured a few unintelligible words to his servant, who bowed low before him for the last time. Snatching the key, Ludwig swiftly reached the door, crossed the great landing and unlocked the door to the spiral-staircase. The next moment he uttered one wild cry ... and stood as if turned to stone.

It had been arranged, as soon as Ludwig appeared, to surround him and carry him off by force. As the King's great dignified figure was seen framed in the doorway, and the keepers prepared to pounce on him to cut off his retreat,——not one of them dared to lay hands on him.

Dr. von Gudden was the first to find his voice. He stepped forward a little and said:

"Your Majesty! Never have I had to break sadder news to anybody than this: After hearing the expert opinion of four brain-specialists on the state of Your

Majesty's health, His Royal Highness Prince Luitpold has felt it to be necessary to assume the regency of Bavaria. I have been commanded to take Your Majesty's health under my care and observation, and I may say that the present moment proves to me without a doubt that, in the interests of Your Majesty's safety, there must be very real reasons for these precautions."

Thus spoke the "terrible" and "hateful" man, bowing low, looking like an actor on the stage. Majestically the King drew himself up to his full height. His tall figure, backed by coloured frescoes, caught the brightness of candlelight, and behind him stretched the vista of gorgeous royal rooms.

Ludwig breathed heavily, straining every nerve to keep himself in control. His poor brothers' ghastly fate rose before his mind's eye, helping him to keep a cool head. But deep down, in the recesses of his soul, he swore death to him who had brought this dastardly message to him.

"What do you require me to do?" he asked, quietly, trying to gain time. "What is the meaning of all this?"

The keepers now advanced to lead him away. With a dignified movement of his hand he waved them off, every inch a king, and drew himself up, saying:

"That is unnecessary: I will go of my own free will"

As he walked back to his bed-room, his step was uncertain; his speech too, was slightly thick, for not only was he suffering from the amount of alcohol he had drunk, but more than all from the shock of the news so cruelly imparted.

"I know what you are going to do, Doctor. Is it quick or slow poison? Speak plainly!"

"Neither the one nor the other, Your Majesty! On the contrary, both Prince Luitpold as well as the whole country, sympathize with Your Majesty and want nothing more sincerely than to see you cured as soon as possible. For this reason it is absolutely necessary for you to leave Neuschwanstein and go to Berg Castle, simply on account of your health——"

"All right, I'm ready to go, I like Berg Castle."

"Then I think the best thing will be for us to go at noce. The carriages are waiting."

"Well, I suppose you won't object to my changing first. Besides which I want to have a word alone with you before we go."

"With pleasure, Your Majesty."

And now the King began a grim game with the man standing before him in feigned reverence, but he must be careful that what he had in mind should escape Gudden's observation.

All the windows of his bed-room had been locked and before each one stood a keeper. Evidently Gudden had prepared for all contingencies. At a word from him the keepers retired, leaving the new "soul-doctor" alone with the King.

"Well, Your Majesty?"

"Oh, drop that word! It's absurd and only bores me. What do you really want? What does all this mean? Speak openly. tell me, what is this plot against me? Have they resorted to this riduculous farce simply to remove me from the government of the country?"

For a moment Gudden had to reflect how best to parry this clever thrust, coming so unexpectedly as it did from a man who was a supposed lunatic. But long years of experience in dealing with the insane decided him to make use of his usual method, to surprise him with the cruel truth. That, thought Gudden, would take the stiffening out of the aristocrat before him.

"Your Majesty is insane and is no longer responsible for your actions. A few moments ago you were intent on committing suicide; yesterday you intended to appear in public in Munich and the day before that you had me and my colleagues imprisoned in the dungeon. We were to be beaten within a inch of our lives, our eyes were to be put out——"

"That's not true; it was only a threat. The light of the eyes is the noblest gift of heaven, as Schiller says in his *"Tell"*.

For a moment the King had forgotten himself, and spoke passionately. Immediately afterwards however, he resumed his self-imposed role of calm aloofness. Gudden took the opportunity to introduce first himself and then each one of his companions by name, which up till now he had omitted to do. Whereupon the King said to Gudden:

"Oh, yes. I remember you quite well and your first audience with me when I appointed you in 1874. You are not a Bavarian."

Again, was that the answer of a lunatic? Such a good memory is a rarity, even amongst the clearest thinkers.

Then the assistant-doctor, Dr. Müller, was introduced and it was noticeable that Ludwig had a struggle to control himself, for this man had up till now been in attendance on the King's unhappy brother. Ludwig pointed towards the table, where the latest report on the health of poor Prince Otto happened to be still lying. He then put the doctor a few questions about the method of treatment in his brother's case, and whilst he listened to the doctor's voice the spectre of his brother's fate rose before him. Suddenly, stopping Müller short in the middle of his report, Ludwig turned again to Dr. Gudden saying:

"What right have you to call me insane when you have neither been attending me nor have you even examined me!"

"Your Majesty, there was no longer any necessity for either the one or the other. We have facts and material enough to support our assertion: indeed, I may say that we have over-powering proofs."

"And how long will it be before I am cured?"

"The Constitution states: should the King be prevented for more than a year from carrying out his duties as a ruler, by any cause whatsoever, a state of regency is to be declared. Consequently a year will be the minimum."

"Couldn't you manage to make it shorter? You could do what they did to the Sultan: it is not at all difficult to get rid of a man."

"My honour forbids me to answer that."

In course of conversation with Dr. Müller, whose regular reports about Prince Otto were always laid before him, the King informed him that he read each report with great attention to detail. Following this he questioned each of the keepers in turn, asking them details about themselves. After each man had answered, Ludwig finished by saying: "But why don't you go? I want to be alone: it's very unpleasant to have so many people in the room."

Each of the keepers answered in the same words, as if it had been drilled into him: "It is the doctor's orders, Your Majesty."

"But Dr. von Gudden, am I to be surrounded by these people all the time at Berg Castle too?"

"That depends entirely when—if ever—Your Majesty becomes quiet enough. Later on it will probably be possible to allow Your Majesty some freedom, perhaps also to walk unguarded in the park at Berg."

"Is then any real possibility of my getting well?"

"For about eighteen months it will not be possible to judge, but I should not like to say that there is no chance of your being cured."

"*Eighteen months*! Thanks very much, Professor! But I don't think it need take as long as that. However, in the meantime we shall become good friends, you may be sure of that, Doctor. You are coming along to Berg too, aren't you?"

"Those were the orders of His Royal Highness, the Prince Regent."

Ludwig was on the point of putting another question,

when he seemed to change his mind, smiled curiously as if at his own thoughts and threw himself heavily onto the edge of his bed.——

Both doctors left him. At a sign from them, the keepers too had gone out of the room, leaving the King alone to change in private. All doors to the room were locked on the outside.

From within came sounds as of sobbing, the hard sobs of age and dispair...

*

A considerable time elapsed before the King reappeared. He came out of his room with a firm tread, dressed in a dark overcoat and a black felt hat. Dawn flickered in the sky: the moment of farewell had come. Before the great portals of the magic castle of Neuschwanstein, a four-in-hand was drawn up.

Dr. von Gudden joined the King. Solemnly, silently, Ludwig went past the model of Falkenstein Castle, his most ambitious project, and crossed the great vestibule. Side by side, Dr. Gudden and he, descended the long flight of steps outside the entrance. Had Ludwig chosen to make use of his well-known bear-like strength it would only have needed one blow and the doctor would have slipped down the stone steps to a certain death. But nothing happened. Collected, composed, without opposition or argument, the King walked out. He entered the carriage on the inside of whose doors there were now no handles—solitary as he had been throughout his whole life. Instead of his coachman Oberholzer, as stranger held the reins and at his side, on the coachman's box, in the place of the usual royal body-guard, sat one of the keepers.

Turning to the doctor, as he took his seat in the carriage, Ludwig said:

"I suppose you've nothing against my saying good-bye to my butler?"

Whereupon Mayr approached the carriage-door, remaining for some time in conversation with the King, who repeated his demand for poison. When at last the butler stepped back from the carriage, he was weeping openly. Meanwhile Dr. Müller with two of the keepers had driven on. Behind Ludwig's carriage came a third, in which were a police-officer, several keepers and Dr. von Gudden. Not a word was spoken.

It was streaming with rain. On the steep serpentine road there were very few persons. As their imprisoned King passed, they raised their hats in silent salute, which he returned in his usual friendly manner. At the bottom of the hill the prisoner, wiping the steam from the window-pane, got one farewell glimpse of his home, before the curve of the road hid it for ever from sight. He gazed his last on that architectural wonder, the work which though representing his still unsatisfied ambition, was a testimony to his ceaseless industry. At that moment his thoughts may well have been: "Will future generations have more understanding for what I, the King, have achieved? Will they reverence these masterpieces and the spirit that inspired them?"

The proud owner had bidden farewell to his castle for

evermore. In the home of his dreams he had suffered dastardly betrayal, had been imprisoned and bereft of his rights. No longer was he king: fled were his day-dreams. He was declared to be the victim of "mental disturbance", for which there only remained life-long incarceration.

Strangely aloof, his will under iron control, Ludwig had allowed himself to be ordered about, had taken this cross upon him like a martyr in a good cause. Yet his royal pride was wounded to the quick; his honour as a German was stained, for he was being treated as a good-for-nothing, as if he were even a danger to his fellow-men.

Not one of all those who held him for insane realized in the least with what clarity and clever logic this solitary man was evolving a means to avenge himself, nor did they suspect that beneath a cloak of well-feigned composure, his heart cried out for revenge.

Reality had laid her rough hand upon this dreamer, thrusting him out into the world, the world that knows no pity. For a little while the King seemed to watch the ghastly spectacle before him, till of a sudden he himself stepped out onto the stage to take the lead in that grim play which was destined to be enacted.

XIII. The Tragedy of Starnberg Lake.

The drive from Neuschwanstein to Berg Castle lasted fully eight hours. For the King, in a closed landau in the heat of a summer day, it was excessively fatiguing, for no one was allowed to converse with him on the way. He was kept in complete seclusion the whole day.

Three times in the course of the drive the horses were changed. At Seeshaupt all Ludwig asked for was a glass of water. The inn-keeper's wife whom Ludwig knew well came curtseying out with the glass of water, but all the King managed to say was just "thank you——thank you——thank you". She who remembered many brilliant royal occasions in by-gone years, began to say something, but was cut short by the coachman whipping up his horses. Bursting into tears the good woman sobbed after the retreating carriage "God help Your Majesty!"

As the four-in-hand swept along the east-shore of Starnberg Lake, a church clock struck twelve.

"Here my life really began——and here it will probably very soon end", Ludwig must have thought to himself.

The new government had given up the idea of sending Ludwig to Linderhof, because their secret informants reported that near Reutte 150 men had been collected together by a royalist game-keeper ready to help Ludwig to escape over the Tyrolese frontier. Had Dr. von Gudden not chosen to take his charge in another direction there is no doubt that they would have been successful in freeing the King. As it was, after two days of fruitless waiting, they were forced to give up their intention and were dispersed.

That Ludwig was taken to where he had spent the first and happiest years of his reign, together with Wagner, Princess Sophie and the Empress of Austria was anything but diplomatic.

A still worse mistake was it to entrust the patient to the care of the director of the public lunatic asylums of Upper Bavaria. They must have known that from having been formerly in attendance on Prince Otto he was too well known to the older brother, who had never liked him. Ludwig had several times spoken about him to his Mother's chief lady-in-waiting and had once said:

"That extraordinary man always watches me with such a suspicious look in his eyes. I only hope he won't find something to say about me too!"

Those of the so-called "Arrest-Commission" who had gone on ahead had arrived in Berg Castle some time earlier and had made all arrangements for the King's arrival. They had taken the handles off the doors, and the fasteners off the windows. Holes had been cut in the doors for purposes of observation, the windows in the second floor had been barred and all heavy articles removed, so that over-night Berg Castle had been changed into a little lunatic-asylum.

With anxiety the members of the Commission watched the carriages coming up the drive. They had been witnesses nearly 15 years before, of their King in the best years of his manhood, in royal splendour.

Was this the same man who stepped out of the carriage broken in nerve and in spirit, complaining of exhaustion and of severe pains in his head? For all present it was a terribly embarrassing moment and each of those who stood there bowing, was assailed with feelings of intense pity mixed with awe. Another stranger was amongst them, Professor Grashey, a world-famous brain-specialist and professor of psychiatry at the University of Würzburg, the son-in-law of Gudden and one of the signatories of the expert report on His Majesty's health. The King greeted no one except the policeman on duty, to whom he said with all his old kindliness:

"Well, Sauer, I'm glad to see you on duty again here!"

On entering the castle, he did not at once notice the changes which had taken place. In one of the first rooms his eye fell upon a large oil-painting representing his first landing at Berg from his steam-launch "Tristan", shortly after his accession. (See plate Nr. 8.) What a gulf separated that day from this! But the pain of this was to some extent mitigated by the genuine pleasure be felt at seeing his old footman Wenzel again.

Arrived in the two rooms above, which had been set apart for him, all he could do was to repeatedly shake his head and murmur to himself: "it won't be long now, my good professor, it won't be long ...!"

He stood in the bow-window gazing thoughtfully down at the surface of the lake. Shimmering white swans passed over it, dreamily, soundlessly. In the distance shone the clear, jagged outline of the Karwendel and Wetterstein ranges, as though they rose sheer out of the blue mist-veiled south-shore. On brilliant green slopes glimmered red roofs of ideally situated country-houses. There also lay Possenhofen where as it happened, though he was not aware of it, Ludwig's former fiancée, the Duchess of Alençon, was staying. As if in the sleep of enchantment slumbered the Isle of Roses, where he had so often met his other cousin, the Empress of Austria. Had Elisabeth, who as usual was spending the summer at Feldafing, found his last letter on the Island, addressed "To the Dove"? Had she perhaps even answered it and left one addressed "To the Eagle"? But no one would ever know that now, for besides themselves no one possessed a key to the writing-table on the Isle of Roses. One thing is certain and is common knowledge, that on the throne of Austria the unhappy daughter of Duke Max tried to forget her first love, Bavaria's handsome young king.

Still Ludwig stood motionless at the window. Today it seemed to him that everything combined in one great symphony of life and death around him. Warm rays from the setting sun caught the burnished surface of the lake. Floating across the water came the voices of holiday-makers, laughing and joking in happy freedom, the most precious of all gifts of which he was now deprived. The transitoriness of all beauty was borne in upon him as never before, filling his aching heart with an inexpressible longing to break the bonds of the living-death with engulfed him. He saw himself a spectre-ship, wrecked upon a blackened strand.

The rooms which had been long unused were full of oppressive heat and bad air. Trying to open the window to get some fresh air, Ludwig realized for the first time the enormity of what had been done to him.——He ground his teeth together in his attempt to control himself, muttering:

"Damn them! They evidently think I'm an absolute lunatic!"

In the middle room on the third floor, a table was set for three persons. Ludwig at once ordered the keepers on duty to clear away two places, as he was accustomed to dine alone. This order was carried out, but all they left him was a basin and a spoon. Knifes and forks were too dangerous to be left with such an irresponsible person!

Later on the doctor requested him to go to bed early. Once more the King obeyed. After he had got into bed, they came and removed his clothes from the room. At first he slept quietly for a few hours, waking at about two o'clock when, as had been his habit for the past few years, he insisted on getting up. This request was refused him and it was only after a great deal of persuasion that one of the keepers was prevailed upon to give him some of his clothes. The rest of that night

Ludwig passed in a half-dressed condition, pacing up and down the room with the bow-window, hour after hour, sleepless and restless, watching the dawn creep greyly through the dense forest surrounding the castle, dreaming of the golden days of care-free youth, aching for the glamour of departed childhood.

*

Von Wobel, the District-Magistrate and Horn, the police-officer were jointly responsible for the guarding of the whole district round the castle. They discussed in all its details certain precautions which were to be taken along the shores of the lake. At the suggestion of Professor Grashey, thin iron rods were to be stuck in along the banks at a slanting angle, which were to be connected by wire-netting to a height of about 6 ft. This would prevent anyone climbing over, yet would not spoil the view over the lake.

The staff of the castle, who were royalist to a man were given strict injunctions that they were not to carry out His Majesty's orders without having first asked permission of one of the gentlemen in authority, who again were to do nothing without consultation with either the chief doctor or his assistant.

Something far more difficult than simply nursing a sick man was in store for these self-sufficient gentlemen: for it had not escaped any one of them that ever since the day Ludwig had been put under guardianship, the man whose brain was said to be "clouded" showed that his power of thinking logically was in no wise impaired, nor did he cease to be the charming yet reserved man he had always been.

*

It was now Whit Sunday, the '13th June, 1886.

At six o'clock in the morning the King asked one of the keepers to prepare him his bath. When he asked for his valet and his hair-dresser, the news was broken to him that they were no longer in attendance on him at Berg. About two hours later, when Ludwig expressed the very natural desire to attend Mass in the neighbouring church, Gudden refused to let him go, fearing that once he had been seen in public the people would cease to believe that their King was really insane!

At 11 o'clock Ludwig invited Dr. Gudden to go for a walk with him. Accompanied by two keepers they strolled along by the lake. At first these men followed quite close behind, till they were told to keep at a somewhat greater distance, meanwhile the King and his doctor sat down on a seat, about 15 ft. from the shore. Ludwig's manner was specially friendly and he spoke without any sign of resentment about his uncle's "coup", maintaining that in his opinion his uncle's hand had been forced by a band of conspirators. Luitpold had always been a man of honour, but had shown himself to be too weak in dealing with intriguers, and incapable of seeing through their manœuvres. That Count Törring had been appointed guardian, met with his entire approval, while the choice of Count Holnstein, the

214

friend of his youth, as his guardian was something he simply could not understand. That the Count had accepted such a post seemed to Ludwig to be incompatible with the very elements of friendship and honour.

Gudden now carefully approached the subject of the treatment that Ludwig was to have, mentioning casually that His Majesty's seclusion could on no account be continued, as solitude was calculated rather to encourage the disease than to cure it. When he named the two gentlemen who had been chosen to be in constant attendance the King answered in a tired voice:

"Even *one* man is too many for me."

From this Gudden, realizing that it would need a long, hard struggle to break his patient's habit of solitude, answered quickly:

"Oh well, at present I think we can allow Your Majesty to be alone; from time to time someone must be in attendance, always for instance when you go for walks in the park, or for an occasional excursion."

"Well, but what about the doctor and the keepers?"

"The doctor as well as the keepers will always knock before entering your room."

"Doctor, I simply couldn't endure such a life. Please let me be alone, except for yourself. I think we understand each other quite well, don't you?"

Gudden felt honoured as well as flattered by this remark, little knowing that a powerful actor, concealed in the soul of the broken man before him, was cleverly fooling and decoying him.

Following this conversation the otherwise so clear-headed director of lunatic-asylums telegraphed to Munich:

"Things going splendidly: is as quiet as a child."

That was the first official report that reached the ministry.

Had the exciting events of the past few days blinded the good doctor, was he after all somewhat embarrassed at having to order the King about, or was it simply that he began to have serious doubts about the truth of his own diagnosis? The assertion that this man was suffering from "insanity" in the form of "paranoia" must be left to modern men of science to confirm or to reject.

As Professor Grashey sat down to write his first official report on the state of his Majesty's health he said quite casually:

"I don't consider the King's case to be incurable!"

"We'll discuss that later!" was the somewhat paradoxical answer of his father-in-law, who looked strangely startled.

At lunch that day Dr. Gudden announced his intention of going to Munich for a few days to get the necessary permits for the treatments he intended to give the King. He added:

"I may say that I have got quite used to His Majesty's ways now, and intend, when I return, to drive and even to go for walks alone with him."

"I wouldn't do that, if I were you. Besides, you would

make my position much more difficult", replied the assistant-doctor, surprised and annoyed.

Had the much younger doctor stronger nerves than his superior? During the drive from Neuschwanstein to Berg the younger man had been obsessed by the fear that the King might suddenly break open the carriage-window, cutting open his artery. Before help could have been brought it might have been all over with Ludwig. Müller's experience with the insane had taught him to dread these sudden suicides. And had not his colleague, who had formerly been his professor, always accentuated in his lectures the need for an almost exaggerated caution in dealing with insane patients, warning his students particularly against going out alone with them? What made Gudden suddenly throw all his theories overboard?

A cloud of ghastly portent hung over Berg Castle, unseen and unsuspected by its inmates!——

*

Towards four o'clock the King took his dinner, again alone. Before sitting down to table he asked the keeper whether Dr. Gudden had done anything to his food, for Ludwig feared that the doctor would give him some stupefying drug and then let people see him, to convince them that their King was really insane.

After dinner Ludwig sent for Dr. Müller.

"At which university did you study?"

"At Würzburg."

"You are a brain-specialist ?"

"Yes, Your Majesty."

"Does your work interest you ? You were in attendance on my brother: how is he now ?"

"His condition has not changed very much during the last few years."

"Well, I suppose that now, instead of sending reports *to* me, you will be making reports *about* me, so you may as well report that I am much worse. People will be glad to hear that !"

"Your Majesty, I am convinced, that everyone will be only too glad to hear that their King's health is improving."

"Tell me, wouldn't it be very easy to put something in my soup so that I should never wake again ?"

(Dead silence on the part of Müller.)

"What sort of sleeping-draughts are there ?"

"Oh, there are lots of different things: for instance opium, morphia, lotions and baths of various sorts, as well as certain gymnastic-exercises."

"You wear spectacles: are you short-sighted ?

"I'm short-sighted in one eye and the other is astigmatic."

"Why is that ? Too much studying ?"

"My eyes were bad even while I was still at school."

"Gudden tells me you would like to re-arrange my library. Do you speak French ?"

"As much as one learns it at school."

"What was your great subject at school ? Are you going to stay on here ?"

"I and another colleague—it is not quite decided who it will be—are to take duty in turns for one month."

"Who will it probably be?"

"No special name has been mentioned."

"Well, whoever he is, he is sure to know of some sort of drug that will polish me off."

"Your Majesty, I can vouch for my colleague as well as for myself. A doctor's duty is to cure, not to kill."

"Yes, I can trust you, but what about that other man?"

In this way harmless, sensible questions such as a man who had been a recluse for years could well have put, alternated with strange remarks intended to feign persecution-mania.

Presently the King nodded kindly, intimating that Dr. Müller could go. Ludwig resumed his usual pacing to and fro. Up and down the room with heavy tread went the tall figure, now extending his arms as if testing his muscles, making curious movements which seemed to indicate some change in his condition.

He now asked to be allowed to have a talk with his old friend Zanders a civil servant. Gudden permitted half an hour's conversation, but on condition that Zanders on no account awakened in Ludwig any hope of his being set free.

The King's manner had undergone a great change: he was very imperious and dictatorial, like he had been in the first years of his reign, utterly different from his manner of the past few days.

"Do you see these bars over the windows, do you see the beastly peep-holes in the doors—do you realize that I'm hedged about with restrictions? Its all simply unheard of!"

In vain Zanders tried to quieten him and to make excuses. The King changed the subject unexpectedly.

"How many policemen are in the park to watch me?"

"Six or eight, Your Majesty."

"In case of need would they shoot me?"

"How could Your Majesty suggest such a thing!"

On the King trying to draw him into a corner of the room in the course of their conversation, Zanders made some excuse and took his leave. Ludwig watched him out of the room with a baffled expression in his eyes.

Dr. Müller meanwhile had gone straight to his superior, Dr. Gudden, and told him all about his curious conversation with the King.

"In my opinion there is something strange in His Majesty's manner, a sort of horrible determination, as if he were following out some definite plan and I feel you ought to be warned."

"My dear young colleague, let the King continue to think that he has gulled me and everybody else. I'm surely experienced enough and have always led my patients by the nose without their having the least suspicion of it. That's the wonderful thing about it, that you can quieten all insane people by apparently giving in to their fantastic notions, and the King is no exception to the rule. We can achieve nothing by argument or opposition. Personally I confess I'm much relieved to see things working out so smoothly."

This distinguished scientist seemed to be blinded by his belief in his infallibility. In spite of Dr. Müller's warning Gudden made arrangements for the King to be temporarily moved into the *Kavalierhaus*, until bars could be fixed to all the castle-windows and the iron-fencing had been made for the shores of the lake.

Professor Grashey and Police-officer Horn went across to Starnberg on business and Gudden told Baron von Washington to either go for a walk or for a drive alone with the King, whichever Ludwig wished, adding that there was no question of the patient being considered a danger to his fellow-men. Washington protested at being expected to go out alone with the King expressing great surprise at Gudden's methods. At that moment one of the servants appeared asking permission to go to Munich at the King's special request, to buy him a new surgical-belt, and Gudden gave his consent with injunctions to the man to report himself early the next morning.

Gudden then expressed his satisfaction to Washington at the way the King was taking everything, falling in with every suggestion, even to being moved to the *Kavalierhaus*, without the least opposition. The King had got hold of the idea, said Gudden, that he was being moved because the castle was to be re-decorated, which was quite a satisfactory solution of the temporary difficulty.

Washington asked Gudden the reason for his changed methods, to which the brain-specialist replied very casually that although his patient often felt very ill, complaining from time to time of the well-known symptom of pains in the back of the head, yet he was very hopeful of being cured. The doctor added that Ludwig's brain was extremely clear and his thoughts logical and correct.

Gudden gave the same sort of report to an American reporter. But when the reporter asked him if it were true that Ludwig was to appear in Munich early on Whit Monday, Gudden exclaimed:

"Stupid nonsense! where did you hear that?"

"From the peasants in the inn at Leoni!"

*

It was late afternoon before the doctor began to prepare for his short absence in Munich. It had slipped his memory that everywhere in Germany the Whitsun week-end was a holiday. After the recent eventful weeks he was looking forward to resting a few days, before taking over the entire responsibilities at Berg Castle. He mentioned incidentally that he would never accept such a responsibility again, even if he were asked to do so and that he had only agreed this time out of a sense of duty to the state.

At this juncture the King sent a request to Gudden to accompany him on a short walk alone, just for an hour before supper. Obviously this was inconvenient for the doctor for he said:

"If only the King will deliver me from these lonely walks in future! The man tires one completely out with all his questions. But I suppose it is not to be wondered at when a man has lived for nearly sixteen years entirely cut off from the society of other men, in self-imposed exile."

In the presence of Maunder, the keeper, Ludwig had changed for the second time that day. He now wore a plain suit with a light summer overcoat and the same soft felt hat to which had been fastened the costly diamond buckle which he had given to his valet Weber.

It was a dull evening, the sky heavy with clouds and a fine rain falling. In spite of this Ludwig asked for his umbrella to be rolled up again and used it as a walking-stick.

The King was only about five paces ahead when Gudden whispered to the keepers:

"No keeper is to accompany us." So the two keepers went back to the castle.

The King and Gudden turned into the same path that they had taken in the morning. Thus fate delivered the doctor into the King's hand. Exactly at 6.25 p.m. the tall figure of Ludwig with the 62-year-old doctor were seen for the last time alive, disappearing from view into the forest. They intended to be back at 8 o'clock at the very latest.

Ludwig knew every inch of the lake-shores from his youth up and it is most probable that during his morning-walk he had chosen the exact spot where he intended to decide his fate.

*

Eight o'clock struck. The two had not yet returned from their walk, though one of them had a train to catch that evening, to Munich.

Professor Grashey and the police-officer were still in Starnberg, the King's valet was in Munich and both the guardians, with Baron Malsen, were in the town on business. Baron von Washington, as the King's personal adjutant and Dr. Müller were left alone in the castle, where they proposed to incarcerate the king whom they called "insane".

Towards 9 o'clock darkness fell. The rain had increased and there was still no sign of the two men.

Could something have happened to them?

In a state of considerable anxiety Dr. Müller walked over from the *Kavalierhaus* to the castle to fetch Dr. Gudden, only to have his anxiety still further increased by being told that His Majesty had not yet returned from his walk.

Out of his mind and left alone in the darkness with a man of 62, beside a great lake and with forest on all sides——it was a simply ghastly thought! And it would not be like Gudden to agree to taking a longer walk than usual at such a late hour. He must know how anxious everyone at the castle would become. Had something happened to the doctor in the forest-park; had the King made his escape——or had they simply walked on to the neighbouring village of Leoni? And if so, what would be the result if the peasants there recognized them?

The assistant-doctor gave orders for the whole of the park to be systematically searched, taking part himself accompanied by the bailiff. At first nobody thought of searching the lake!

Left now quite alone in the castle, Baron Washington tried to keep a cool head, refusing to fear the worst and taking every precaution to prevent the news of what was going on at the castle from reaching the outside world. His thought flew to the thousands of happy holi-day-makers celebrating Whitsuntide in the neighbourhood. If they knew that anything had happened to their beloved King there would be talk of foul play and they would attack any official they met. Should alarmist news reach the capital, there might be a revolution! Not only the lives of the guardians of His Majesty, but of the cabinet and even of the Prince Regent himself would be in danger, for they would become victims of an angry mob.

The preliminary search having brought no result, the entire staff of the castle were now requisitioned in an organized patrol of the whole park-lands, with instructions to each man that should he see the King he was to conceal himself immediately.

There now ensued many minutes of suspense, but this second search also ended negatively. Only then did the idea take shape that an accident might have taken place on the shores or in the lake itself. Dr. Müller proposed to have the lake dragged by some of the fishermen, but Washington advised him against doing this, fearing that too many people would become involved in the search and get to know that something serious was on foot. Also he could not bring himself to believe that anything could have happened in the water, as he had noticed many small boats going to and fro between Starnberg and Leoni during the evening, which would surely have noticed anything unusual or have heard any cries for help.

Zanders meanwhile had fitted out each of the men-servants with a torch and lantern, so that at any rate the actual shores could be searched more thoroughly. Another tense quarter of an hour passed. No sign was found to give any clue.

Washington now felt that the time had come to communicate with the Prince Regent and the gentlemen of the Cabinet. First he wired to his superior, Colonel Freyschlag and then to the Cabinet, confidentially, not officially.

Hardly had these unofficial telegrams been dispatched than some of the police guarding the park came in to report that right through the centre of a meadow they had found wheel-traces of a carriage heading for Munich, although the carriage-gates of the drive were locked.

What could that mean? Had Ludwig after all carried

out the escape he had planned at Neuschwanstein ? Had that "imbecile" coachman, Osterholzer, who had secretly informed Ludwig of the arrival of the so-called Arrest-Commission at Hohenschwangau, managed with the help of his consorts to persuade the King to slip away to Munich ? Had this man successfully carried out what Count Dürckheim had failed to accomplish ? The King himself was certainly too ill to have undertaken such a *coup* on his own initiative, but it was of course not impossible if accomplices had decoyed Dr. Gudden away, leaving him lying dead in some bushes, that Ludwig would no longer have hesitated to enter a waiting carriage. At this very moment he was probably in Munich: perhaps the revolution had already broken out and all their lives were in danger ! Why had that American reporter asked such a strange question: whether it was true the King was going to appear at the Palace on Whit Monday ?

Washington was in a quandary and for the moment he knew not how to act for the best. A false step at this juncture might have the gravest results in the country. However, his worst fears abated somewhat on hearing from Dr. Müller who entered the room at that moment, that the coachman Osterholzer had been arrested some time before for grave insubordination, being held responsible for the disagreeable affair of the imprisonment and subsequent return to Munich of the first Commission.

Accordingly Washington sent a precautionary telegram to the Chief of Police Pechmann in Munich:

"His Majesty and Dr. Gudden went out at 6.30——not yet returned——park being searched."

That was the second official telegram from Berg Castle. Washington would have liked to advise Pechmann to patrol all roads to Starnberg with mounted-police, but at the last moment he thought better of it. After all, Pechmann as chief of police of the third largest city in Germany would read between the lines and know best what to do.

To Baron Crailsheim a private wire was sent as follows:

"A reporter asked this evening whether His Majesty is really appearing to-morrow morning in Munich—valet asked leave to-night to go to Munich, which was granted."

Was it not rather a curious coincidence that the valet should have been sent so late in the evening to buy something for His Majesty? He should really have been followed to see where he went to. Perhaps he never went to Munich at all, but was simply preparing plans for the King's escape. Or he may have slipped over to Feldafing to the Empress of Austria, carrying important messages from Ludwig.

These two telegrams had only just gone off when there were sounds of great excitement in the castle below. A footman had brought in the King's hat which he had found at the water's edge. It was drenched with lake-water and badly torn.

A few minutes later searchers came in, bringing other

unmistakeable proofs that a terrible fate had overtaken the two missing men, for another of the men-servants had found Dr. Gudden's hat and the King's overcoat and jacket lying near the shore, all of them wet through. The strange thing was that Gudden's hat was crushed right in and that all these articles were not actually in the water, but close by, on the shore. A little further off, lying near the seat upon which Ludwig and the doctor had sat that morning, the umbrella was found.

It was clear that a ghastly tragedy had taken place, which being restricted to two victims, precluded all possibility of other lives being in danger, which was a meagre consolation.

Huber, the bailiff, together with Dr. Müller, jumped into a boat to search the shallows near the shore, when their voices were heard simultaneously crying:

"There !——There they are !——"

Not far from land they had come upon the body of Dr. Gudden in a half-sitting posture, his back under water and at a short distance from him the corpse of the King, wearing no jacket, face downwards and with his arms stretched out, both bodies floating on the surface. In each case it seemed that their feet had been caught in the mud on the bottom of the lake. (See plate 32.)

Wolb, one of the horse-trainers, hurried up to the castle with the fateful news: "we have found the bodies of His Majesty and the doctor in the lake".

Though half anticipating such a possibility, Washington was greatly shocked at the news. His first act was to wire to Colonel Freyschlag, the members of the Cabinet and the chief district judge at Starnberg. That was the third official telegram from Berg Castle.

He then hurried down to the lake-shore. On the way he was met by the butler and the head-cook who exclaimed:

"His Majesty and Dr. Gudden are both showing faint signs of life !"

They both assured Washington that this was true and were even ready to take their oath upon it, saying they had seen it with their own eyes. Washington therefore turned back to the castle to send off this report word for word, to Munich.

That was the fourth telegram to the Cabinet.

*

Both the bodies were laid on the shore. The King's watch dangled from his waistcoat pocket and had stopped at 6.54; water had got in between the glass and the face of the watch.

Whilst two policemen tried to restore breath to the body of Gudden, Dr. Müller and a third policeman did all that was humanly possible to bring the King back to life, removing his shirt to be able to apply friction, for which the good fellow Zanders quickly cut pieces of cloth from his own jacket. Not until then did it occur to them to send up to the castle for blankets. Every few moments rain and wind threatened to extinguish the lanterns, their wavering flame adding much to the misery of the tense little group on the shore.

In vain Dr. Müller attempted to resuscitate the King
—in vain were the efforts of the others. Not wanting
to bring the dead to the castle in a boat, a carriage was
ordered to come right down to the water's edge.

At midnight Dr. Müller at last rose from his knees
beside the King's body and turning to Baron von Washington
who stood beside him, said:

"Baron, there is no more hope! We can do nothing
more: we've tried everything—it is too late!"

Each of the doctor's words fell like blows on fresh
wounds. A bitter sense of disaster assailed the true-
hearted little group, whilst wavelets born of the night-
wind broke shudderingly at their feet. The tragic truth
had been put into words, a truth that none dared to face:
the dead were beyond recall.

A telegram was now sent by Baron Washington to
the Prince Regent himself, as he assumed that by the
time it would be delivered, Colonel Freyschlag, as well
as the entire Cabinet, would be assembled in audience
with the Prince Regent.

No carriage was brought from the castle; instead,
they laid the bodies one at each end of a boat. Slowly
they steered the little boat with its sad burden up towards
the castle, the King with his face turned towards his
beloved park and Dr. Gudden with his gaze towards the
wild water.

Poor Gudden! In spite of everything, he was to be
pitied. For his inexcusable document declaring the King
to be insane, for his conceited belief in his own scien-

tific experience and infallibility, he had been called upon to pay the uttermost penalty!

Poor Ludwig! Far more are you to be pitied! To this dark hour have they driven you, who tore you from the glamour of your solitude! It is finished! Your soul has reached its longed-for goal, has entered into the Eternity of its Walhalla.

These two men so peacefully lying opposite one another, who but a few short hours before must have been in the grip of a deadly death-struggle, was a heart-breaking, unforgettable sight.

In the sleep of death they returned to the castle, to be swathed in sheets and to lie all through that sunny Whit-Monday morning, never more to awaken.

All the complicated preparations, the precautionary measures, and the secretive planning to circumvent an unpractical dreamer, seemed now like a ghastly dance of death, a dance that the great-souled recluse himself had seen fit to bring to a sudden close. The silence of eternity had fallen.

Four official telegrams had been sent to Munich and as many unofficial ones had been dispatched to different ministers, but up till now no single word of reply had been received from Munich.

At 2 a.m. the chief district-judge came over from Starnberg, accompanied by a doctor and the coroner. The result of their inspection of the bodies was as follows:

"Dr. Guddens face showed a number of scratches on

the forehead and nose; a deep cut on the forehead caused by a blow from a stick; over his right eye a bruise of considerable size, the result of a blow; a cut on his right cheek; the nail of the middle finger of the right hand badly torn and marks of strangulation round the neck. No marks of any kind on His Majesty's body, but a strangely sinister, tyrannical look on his face."

Entirely contradictory to the above report regarding the King's expression in death was that of Prince Philipp zu Eulenburg, secretary to the Prussian Embassy in Munich, who writes:

"... with beating heart I entered the room where the mythical King, the smile of insanity on his pale lips, his ivory-white brow framed in waves of strong black hair, had just been laid upon his death-bed."

Which is true? The sinister, tyrannical expression or the smile of insanity?

*

From Munich came absolutely no news whatsoever. Nevertheless the adjutant of the dead king carried out his sad and difficult duties, of which the next was to telegraph to the Countess von der Mühle, chief lady-in-waiting to the Queen-Mother, who was in Elbingalp:

"Prepare Her Majesty for the news that the King is dead."

The faithful Baron von Washington had gone through a terrible night of strain, but had never faltered in his duty. He had sent telegrams in every direction, taking endless pains in the wording of each, that it should be.

clear, stating facts without being alarmist. He felt the intense responsibility of his position at such a juncture, but nobody in Munich felt it incumbent upon him to send him an answer. No word of regret, no instructions——nothing !

On his enquiring at the Munich Post-Office he received the answer: "all messages delivered". He had even taken the precaution to send a carriage to Fürstenried, feeling certain that at least Count Holnstein would come up from Munich, but the carriage waited there in vain.

At last—towards 5.30 a.m.—Count Törring arrived to relieve Baron Washington. But not until three hours later did Baron Malsen, accompanied by a certain *Hofrat* Klug and the secretary of the Queen-Mother, put in an appearance. Washington asked:

"What did the Prince Regent say to my telegram ? I hardly know myself, now, what I said in my wire to him."

"They waked him" was Malsen's laconic answer. This answer is typical of the man himself. Reserved and unbending in manner, he never trusted himself to be natural for fear of giving himself away on some subject of importance. Washington, very indignant at such an insolent, insufficient reply, turned brusquely to *Hofrat* Klug with the question:

"When did Colonel Freyschlag receive my first message ?"

"At 12.30 all three telegrams were handed to him together."

"To me that appears simply inconceiveable ! That the adjutant of His Majesty the King of Bavaria should telegraph to the chief-adjutant of His Royal Highness the Prince Regent at 9.30 p.m., to communicate news of the utmost importance to the country and that such a message should have taken over three hours to reach Munich from Berg ! No one can make me believe that ! I shall protest about this and have the matter thoroughly gone into. That the railway-officials should have been guilty of such arrant neglect of their duties appears at first sight to be a sheer impossibility."

"Lieut.-Colonel, I must beg you——"

"Very well, but please tell me this : the telegrams reached Colonel Freyschlag half an hour after mid-night. What did he do then ?"

"He sent me to communicate the three messages to the Cabinet, which, although after mid-night, were still in session, but the Prince Regent himself was not present."

"Well then, who waked His Royal Highness ?"

"The Cabinet dispersed at about 1.30, to reassemble at 7 a.m. They instructed me to send them further details of what has happened from here."

"I see. So it was not even considered necessary to summon the Prince Regent to be present at such an important Cabinet Meeting ! What has been happening here seems to be of little importance to these gentlemen ! The whole country is in a state of the greatest excitement already, but perhaps in the meantime they may have seen fit to wake the Prince Regent !"

"Your Excellency! I must really beg you once more—"

It is very certain that no one was prepared for this kind of treatment and at such a moment, from a representative of the government, least of all the dead King's personal adjutant. He had naturally assumed that the Cabinet would at least have communicated with him direct in the course of their meeting, requesting him personally to supply details of what had taken place. Instead of which they sent this man called Klug as their representative, who until a few weeks previously had been simply an obscure theatre-superintendent.

Under such humiliating conditions it will be readily understood that Baron Washington refused to discuss the matter further with such representatives from Munich, and that he abruptly turned and left the room.

*

By 10 o'clock that morning the two bodies had been placed in different rooms, separated by a little sitting-room. All three rooms were already filled with masses of flowers. Outside the castle a great crowd had gathered of tourists, Whitsuntide holiday-makers and peasants, all wanting to see their beloved king once more, so that police had to guard the entrance.

As one of the first whom the sad news had reached, came Elisabeth from Feldafing. The tragic end of her dear friend, in whose "insanity" she had never believed, shook her to the roots of her being. On seeing the still form she was distraught with grief, sobbing convulsively:

"He is not really dead! My dear, dear Ludwig! It is only pretence: all he wants is to be left in peace——not to be persecuted any longer!"

She requested her ladies-in-waiting to leave her alone by the death-bed, on the pillow of which she laid a deep-red rose. (See plate 33.) After a considerable time, her attendants hearing no sound from within, re-entered the death-chamber, to find Elisabeth lying unconscious beside the bed. Baron Washington was later on requested to lay a magnificent wreath which she sent to Munich, on the coffin in the Old Chapel.

It was now mid-day on Whit Monday and not one single member of the Cabinet had yet arrived.

Not until 4 o'clock that day did Crailsheim, together with several others in mourning-coats arrive, to make final arrangements for transferring the body of the King to Munich.

Ludwig, who so often in the last few days had been forced to make a pretence to blind others, could now pretend no longer. He who in his lifetime had laid so much stress on dignity, was carried in no dignified manner by four grooms down the great staircase, to where his coffin awaited him. Neither members of the royal family, nor the master of the ceremonies were present.

The sad little procession, headed by priests, moved out of the castle-gates, to the sounds of uncontrolled sobbing from the crowd that watched them go. It passed through Fürstenried, where the insane brother Otto, in the bloom of his manhood, was pining away his days.

At Sendling a squadron of light-cavalry was met, which formed a guard of honour, while great crowds of country-people followed the coffin into the town.

As the dead man re-entered the walls of the palace he so much hated, a shudder passed over the silent crowds. A never-ending train of people passed through the Old Chapel (see plate 34), within whose walls Ludwig had conferred upon so many the Knighthood of St. George, to take one last look on the King's enigmatical expression in death. There, on a simple catafalque, lay the mortal remains of their King, wearing the uniform of the Knights of St. Hubertus. One of his long shapely hands rested upon the hilt of his sword, while the other, holding a little bunch of white jasmine picked and placed there by Elisabeth, lay across his breast. Only she knew that next to lilies and roses, jasmine was the favourite flower of her beloved friend Ludwig. That the meaning of the persian-arabic word "jasmine" was "despair", she neither knew at the time, nor did she realize it later. (See plate 35.)

Thousands followed the coffin to the royal crypt in St. Michael's Church, to the sombre tolling of many bells and the monotonous chant of the priests. Following the coffin came the Prince Regent, the Crown Prince Rudolf of Austria and the German Crown Prince Friedrich of Prussia.

To the deep tones of the Benno-bell in the tower of the *Frauenkirche* the Bavarian people and the whole German nation mourned for this noblest of all princes, who had passed into eternity. It was not only the simple people who mourned him, who thought of him still as the brilliant youth in regal robes of twenty years ago, but all circles of that Munich society which Ludwig had latterly so assiduously avoided, high and low, rich and poor, were filled with an intense pity.

On all the highest peaks of the alps, on the great heights of the Säuling, on the rocks of St. Magnus, flickered the flames of St. John's Day fires, funeral-piles to Baldur, the god of light. The silence of death enveloped the castles of Neuschwanstein and Hohenschwangau. At half-mast hung the flags over Linderhof and Herrenchiemsee. Never would the solitary King re-enter their doors, nor would the solitude into which he had now entered ever again be broken. From all the castles happiness had fled, for neither wife nor child had Ludwig left behind him.

Whilst in the town the mortal remains of Ludwig were laid to rest in the crypt of his fathers, through the whole country-side the air vibrated to the grave-song of a thousand tolling bells.

And for the last time in his honour, the echoes awoke to the thunder of cannons.

XIV. Legend and Truth.

After Ludwig II. of Bavaria had met with such an untimely end, the opinion of German historians of that period could be summed up in the following sentences:

"The second Ludwig, who was out of his senses, wasted his own and his people's money in morbid passions and costly buildings; in insanity he ended his own life and that of his doctor. His successor, King Otto, who is also out of his mind, is under guardianship and the government of the country is in the hands of a Regent. In the modern state, it is never the inclinations of the King, but the well-being of the whole nation which must be the decisive factor."

Countless legends of the strangest kinds have gathered round the story of Ludwig, making such inroads on the structure of actual facts, that to-day is no longer easy to distinguish fact from fancy.

The two decisive questions both at the time and now are: How did he die and was he really out of his mind?

*

How did he die? What really happened and how did it happen?

There were no eye-witnesses. All we have to go on are indications. In any attempt to form a judgement on the matter by carefully weighing pros and cons, we have nothing but indications to depend on.

240

Did the King only try to commit suicide? Did he only try to escape, simply to get out of prison? Did he seize the doctor and drag him into the water, to intentionally strangle or drown him? Or did Dr. von Gudden jump in after him in an attempt to prevent the King from committing suicide? Was Gudden victim of a heart-attack? Was the King's death a natural one or did he drown in full possession of his senses?

One thing is quite certain that right from the beginning of the last stage leading to the actual tragedy, Ludwig's mind was obsessed by three different thoughts, which followed one another in quick succession: resistance (appeal for help to the neighbouring villages, arrest of the first Commission, his orders to Count Dürckheim and the Kempten Rifle-battalion, his last proclamation to the country); then flight (his discussion with Dürckheim, his order to Osterholzer which came too late); and lastly, suicide (talks with his valets, cyanide of potassium, key to the tower and his attempt to fling open the window just as Mayr entered).

It was not until the moment when he was so brutally surprised on opening the door to the spiral-staircase that the fourth and far more terrible thought took hold of him on seeing Dr. Gudden, that of revenge. This idea of revenge, Ludwig concealed in a truly masterly manner, only on occasions of sudden excitement giving even the faintest indication of what was in his mind: for instance the King's question to the doctor: "What right have you to call me insane when you have not even examined me" which he repeated with such insistence at Berg Castle. Also that strange exclamation which he made must have some deeper meaning when he said: "I shall render account to heaven and to the *Vogt*!" Who else could he have meant by "*Vogt*" than his "*appointed tamer*", Dr. von Gudden?

His first idea of resistance he relinquished when Dürckheim was summoned to Munich and when the expected 300 riflemen failed to appear, with whom he had intended to defend his castle to the last. Resistance fled too, when he himself finally gave up the idea of returning to Munich.

On the other hand the thought of suicide was given up at the moment of leaving Neuschwanstein, which was after the doctors and keepers had been sprung upon him. Had he really still thought of committing suicide, it would have been very easy for him, whilst changing in private, to have hung himself, or during the drive to Berg in the closed carriage to have broken the windows and cut open both his arteries. In both cases help would have come too late, as Dr. Müller himself had said, for the King with his herculean strength would have successfully prevented all attempts to rescue him.

On arrival at Starnberg Lake, only revenge or flight occupied his thoughts. These thoughts indeed took more and more definite shape as Ludwig realized one after the other the depressing and humiliating changes that his beloved castle had undergone. From that time onwards he had the thought of his brother's incurable disease before his mind and was obsessed by one single desire, to be alone with Gudden!

On Whit Sunday morning he had half succeeded in what he planned. The only thing that stood in his way on that first walk in the park, was the presence of two keepers following close behind, and the fact that it was day-light. He saw that it would be wiser to wait for the twilight and then quite casually to suggest a walk without the keepers. This he did and his suggestion was acted upon. No doubt Dr. Gudden thought to do the King a special favour in granting this wish, hoping to facilitate matters for himself later on in his difficult task of treating the invalid and winning his confidence.

It is extraordinary that many things that happened during the few days before the tragedy, which were grave indications, seem to have passed unnoticed by one who, like Dr. Gudden, was considered to be a shining-light in his profession. For instance Ludwig never asked to see any of his numerous relatives, gave up making any entries in his diary and repeatedly asked for cyanide of potassium, even asking what other poisons might possibly be administered to him without his knowledge. He also made stipulations about the method of treatment to be pursued and asked how long it would take, all of which were questions intended to distract the attention of those in attendance on him. Finally, pursuing the same tactics, he cleverly contrived to send his valet into Munich, ostensibly to buy him something.

And so it came about that the King went out again

towards evening with Dr. Gudden. No doubt he turned the conversation into channels of general interest, mentioning too that they must not forget to be back in time for an early supper that night on account of the doctor's visit to Munich, asking him also to do one or two little things for him while he was in town. Meanwhile he led his companion towards that part of the shore which he had chosen that morning. He, as a strong swimmer, remembered from former years that at this point the lake was only waist-deep. Whether the two sat down again on the bench on which they had sat that morning, can not be proved.

By this time Ludwig must have noticed that no keepers were following them and would have expressed his appreciation of this fact to Dr. Gudden in a few grateful words. Following this he doubtless asked the doctor the same question that he had put to Zanders a few hours earlier, about the number of guards placed around the park and their position, to which in all probability he will have received an answer which set his mind at rest on this subject.

Suddenly he will have reverted to the subject of the disgraceful doctor's certificate declaring him to be out of his mind. With all the imperiousness of which he was capable he will have demanded to be set free from all restrictions. Gudden, though tremendously startled and fully aware of the dangers involved, must have categorically refused this, with the firmness born of his long experience in dealing with the insane. The doctor's energetic opposition, which would have reduced a man whose brain was really "disordered" to a state of apathy, had just the contrary effect on the King's sound common sense.

Just as suddenly and unexpectedly Ludwig now took the law into his own hands. With lightning rapidity, with a terrible oath the King must have dealt the doctor a stunning blow. (Proof: the deep wound on Gudden's forehead.)

The doctor was beyond shouting for help: his hat fell off and lay at his feet. The suddenness of the blow left him entirely helpless; dazed and half-unconscious he sank to the ground, his whole weight resting on his hat. (Proof: the hat which was found so strangely pressed together, as if it had been subjected to great weight.)

His freedom had been refused, his revenge on Gudden had been taken and for the moment the King was rid of him. Should a keeper suddenly appear from some hiding-place, he too would have to be rendered unconscious by a blow.

But no keeper appeared. An uncanny silence enveloped the lonely man, only broken by the uneven gasping of the unconscious figure at his feet. No call for help had been given, no guards appeared. Ludwig however, realized that his freedom was only partial, as escape through the park, which he had primarily intended, had now become, without Gudden's help, an impossibility. The sentries guarding the park would never let him pass unaccompanied.

A fine misty rain made itself felt. Before him little restless wavelets broke on the shore unceasingly. His sudden freedom from doctor, keepers and guards made Ludwig's clear brain work with increased rapidity. In these last moments before his death an intense and overwhelming desire for life swept through him with the force of an avalanche. His great strength which had only been put to the test in the one blow given to Gudden, was still unimpaired. Now was the time for him, formerly a champion-swimmer, to swim the lake and make one last attempt to regain his liberty. There lay the Isle of Roses, and close by was Possenhofen. The distance at the narrowest part was not quite $1\frac{1}{5}$ miles as he knew well. How often had he swum the Alpsee at Hohenschwangau, which was just the same distance, without the least fatigue. He had heard too, that Elisabeth was staying over there. She who had always stood by him, would do so now and help him, if necessary, over the frontier to Austria.

His breath rattling painfully, Gudden still lay where he had fallen. The King took off his overcoat, threw his hat down and then took off his jacket as well. It might hinder him in swimming. Turning to give one last look round him, he trod on the brim of his hat. Then he waded out into the water.

At that moment the doctor must have come to himself, seen what was happening and gathering his last strength together have sprung up, urged by a stern sense of duty and with only one thought uppermost, to save the King at all costs. There was no moment to be lost. It probably never occured to him that it might be simply an attempt on the King's part to escape alive. All that the doctor saw was the frightful sight of one about to commit suicide, and he sprang into the water to the rescue.

About 20 ft. from the shore he reached the King, who turned and half in anger, half in despair, dealt him a tremendous blow in the face. (Proof: the great bruise above the doctor's right eye.) But this did not deter the doctor from his self-imposed duty. He clung to his master like a vampire, in his attempt to prevent the worst. In the mind of the other only one thought prevailed, born of self-defence: to destroy the "miserable fellow" who had condemned him to a living-death and who was now trying to frustrate even this last bid for life. He must strangle him! The doctor did not deserve any better fate and now he should meet his death at the hand of his King. In blind fury he reaches out for Gudden's head time after time, scratching his cheek repeatedly in his efforts to seize hold of him. Farther and farther the two drifted out to sea in their death-grapple. No help is to be expected. In the hand to hand struggle the King almost tears the nail from his opponent's right hand, grasping him at last with the strength of a lion in a strangle-grip.

Half drowned, half suffocated——the fateful hour strikes. Suddenly the King's grip loosens. A second before like an animal at bay, caught in a trap and surrounded by its enemies, he had struck out. The next moment his

great shoulders, risen high out of the water, submerge——
struck by apoplexy! The tragedy was not the King's
arbitrary act as most people think. Death stepped between
him and his attempted escape. That shortly before leaving
the castle he had had a meal, the post-mortem examination
proved without a doubt. On a full stomach the King
had plunged into the cold lake and abnormal perspiration
had ensued, owing to the superhuman exertion of the
struggle in the water. That which a healthy man could
hardly endure, was too much for the weakened constitution
of the 41-year-old King.

They were both dead, but neither could they sink nor
drift away, for both had their feet too deeply sunk in
the sand. They were found as described, each with just
the head and shoulders floating. To drown or to try to
drown oneself, at the particular spot where, a few hours
later, the bodies were found, is an absolutely impossible
proposition, for the water is only waist-high.

Just as impossible is it, that the King committed suicide.
Quite apart from the fact that suicides very rarely talk so
openly about their plans, as Ludwig had done for the
last five years of his life, and that as a strong swimmer
he would be the last man to choose the terrors of death
by drowning, having had a choice of easier ways of ending
his life at Neuschwanstein, there are many other indications for rejecting the supposition that he took his own
life. Why, for instance, if Ludwig proposed to drown
himself, did he remove his overcoat, jacket and hat?

Why did he send his servant to Munich to buy him a new surgical-belt, unless he intended to go on living? Why did he ask to be informed of the exact position of the sentinels posted around the confines of the park? Why did he submit to being taken to Berg Castle at all, as if he were an invalid?

That Ludwig did not throw himself into the water like any ordinary suicide, straight from the shore or from the seat, is proved by his clothing found on the shore. That he did not simply escape suddenly from his companion, like a man who is completely out of his mind and has no lucid moments, is proved by the foot-marks which show a short struggle between the two men. Again, that such a struggle can only have taken place before he entered the water is clear and explains Gudden's crushed hat and the wound on his forehead, which could only have been made by a stick, the stick in this case being the King's umbrella. In the water Ludwig had nothing in his hand, for the servants found his umbrella on the shore.

On the other hand it is extremely unlikely that the King seized Gudden and dragged him into the water, as he would have had to reckon with the appearance of one of the keepers, for in such a case Gudden would have shouted for help. The only question which remained unanswered is, did the doctor meet his death by suffocation or by drowning. No one will ever be able to answer this, as strangely enough, no post-mortem examination was made of the body of Gudden (why was this omitted?).

When therefore, owing to the very distinct signs of strangulation found on the doctor's neck we assume that he met his death in this way, we must understand and condone the fact from the point of view that it was humanly natural for the King to feel himself deeply humiliated at such treatment from a subject and that if he acted thus at the last minute, he did so in self-defence.

Certain it is that in the hour of death, neither of the two men were wanting in courage, for Gudden too had sacrificed his life to the state. To rescue the life confided to his care, he gave his own. In justice to him, let this be remembered!

When the events of the 13th June 1886 became known, it was the general opinion throughout Germany that the Bavarian King had sought and found his death by drowning. But discussing the question nowadays in Upper Bavaria as to whether or not their King took his own life, you get nothing from these healthy-minded peasants but a shake of the head and a flat denial. Yet nearly all of Ludwig's biographers roundly reject the theory that he was merely attempting to escape, some trying to explain what happened in the following manner: "had the King wished, he knew of paths through the forest and along the lake-shores that offered him chances enough to escape from Gudden and reach those who awaited him outside the park——why therefore should he have chosen to attempt a haphazard flight by swimming the lake?"

Consequently, supporters of the above theory would have us believe that Ludwig was ignorant of the existence of either keepers or of the sentinels stationed at intervals right round the park and who would certainly have prevented his escape. That this was not the case we however know, for the "prisoner" had very carefully informed himself of the exact whereabouts of the sentinels. And could it really be called a "haphazard" attempt at flight, had he swum the lake? It is true, that Duke Ludwig denied the rumour that he awaited the King with his carriage on the other side of the water, but how did it stand with Elisabeth, of whom it was said that the "Empress Elisabeth had sent out a boat from Feldafing to meet her cousin?" Did the Empress ever deny this rumour? One in her position would be compelled to publicly deny such a rumour of intended help, had there really been no truth in it——which denial was never made. Why was this? And was the valet really sent into Munich to buy a belt? On the other hand, what was going on at Hohenschwangau? Did the 150 men on the Austrian frontier await developments for fully forty-eight hours for their own amusement? And did not the Austrian authorities near the frontier seriously reckon with the possibility of the Bavarian King's escape, when they applied to head-quarters in Vienna for instructions for such an event taking place? Lastly, did all the many little boats that crossed the lake that afternoon do so on such a rainy day merely for pleasure?

To a certain extent the biographers are right that there

are no proofs with which to support any theory. But one must also remember that the new government would have imprisoned anyone for high-treason who had produced proofs which might have upset their carefully-worded official reports of the tragedy.

Few are capable of giving an opinion of any value on this much debated question. It is however historically interesting to read the summing up of *Geheimrat* Dr. Fritz Jolly, one of the greatest authorities on psychiatry of the Berlin University. He writes:

"Significant of the King's condition is the fact that in conversation with Dr. Müller he showed a certain degree of cunning, endeavouring to get information out of him by indirect means as to whether they were planning to poison him, assuring him that he trusted him but not the other doctor. Probably he gave Gudden the same assurance. That at the time of his leaving the castle the King was intent on either escape or suicide is, in my opinion, absolutely certain. If therefore, the events in question were simply an attempt on his part to escape, *which I consider is not impossible*, the King would have been ..... etc."

Completely untrue is the rumour that the government intended to get rid of the King by force. Scandal-mongers circulated just as untrue a story when they said that his new adjutant, Baron von Washington, had instructions to give His Majesty every possible assistance in making his escape. On the contrary, just the opposite was the case, for Washington proved by his many telegrams to

Munich that he was almost over-conscientious in his new office. It was the government itself that showed the utmost indifference to the events which presaged the end of the monarch they had taken steps to render harmless. That is the whole truth, however bitter it may sound in the ears of a Ministry !

*

This brings us to the other great question: was Ludwig II. really mad or did he only suffer from time to time from fixed ideas that made of him merely an eccentric?

As has been shown, the King was not declared to be mad by the Bavarian people, but solely by his Cabinet and on the strength alone of the diagnosis of a state-doctor. The pivot upon which the whole royal tragedy turns is this diagnosis. Let us look back and consider impartially how it originated and the events that led up to it. The birthright of even the lowliest in a civilized state, to which every murderer has a claim, i.e. the right to be examined as to his mental condition——was withheld from Ludwig of Bavaria, the greatest in Germany after the Emperor. Prince Luitpold had indeed expressed the wish for a personal examination of the King, but four brain-specialists, by virtue of the damning evidence in their possession, declared this to be superfluous. These "proofs" of supposed madness consisted of documents collected by the doctors containing evidence given on oath by the King's servants. In the experts' opinion, this sufficed !

While Professor Grashey considered the King's

condition to be curable if he could have been put under treatment earlier in life, *Hofrat* Hagen declared a cure to be absolutely hopeless in the case of members of a family with hereditary taint.

Dr. Hubrich, director of a lunatic asylum, diagnosed the unhealthy condition of mouth and teeth as an extremely significant symptom, whereas any dentist would have recognized it as poverty of blood. Anaemic people suffer very often from headaches and sleeplessness, for which doctors prescribe to this day pain-stilling medicine and sleeping-tablets. Just because Ludwig II. took these medicaments, it did not prove that he was mad. Yet Dr. Hubrich even went further, opining that the King, with his lack of real musicality, had only become enthusiastic for Richard Wagner's compositions because the Wagner operas, in their fantastic beauty, acted as a stimulant to his brain !——

Let us now consider the evidence of the servants. First and foremost of these was of course that of the butler Mayr, whose contribution included the following: "His Majesty loses control of his limbs at times, being capable in anger of dancing a demoniacal dislocated kind of dance, ghastly to see, beating the air with his arms like a wild man. For want of anything better to do he sometimes sits for hours twirling a lock of his hair between his fingers or passing the comb through it. At table he drops the gravy about on the table-silver like a small child, and once during a severe attack of persecution-mania he ordered a knife to be removed from the table which should have lain there, but which actually was missing that day. When the thermometer is well below zero he takes his meals out of doors, going for walks in the warmest weather with an over-coat and umbrella. During the last twelve months orders were given only through the closed door, servants in his presence being required to make signs without speaking a word and in a bowed position. Anything they have misunderstood must be written down on paper in the ante-room. Should a servant be guilty of some mistake, he is required to show his respectful apology by bowing down flat on the floor after the manner of the Chinese court. Neither whilst waiting at table nor when valeting is the master to be looked at." Mayr furthermore swore that he himself, for a year or more, had only been allowed to appear wearing a black mask, because the King could no longer bear the sight of a robust face in the rarefied atmosphere in which he lived.

One man-servant called Buchner gave evidence that he was made to wear a seal hanging in front of his forehead, as a sign of his denseness and general inadequacy.

Another man-servant called Sauer was to be set upon a donkey, dressed in some bright-coloured robe and to be made an exhibition of in the street, because of "bestial idiocy" (of course this threat was never carried out!). "During those nights when the King was awake, anyone who fell asleep would get spit in the face".——

Such stories and others still worse, formed the material which was put at the disposal of the experts by uneducated or half-educated persons from amongst the King's staff, two of whom were former court-secretaries. These witnesses were those who had either found disfavour with the King, or were bribed. The greater part of what they reported, as has been proved without a doubt, consisted of gross misrepresentations, exaggerations and misunderstandings, as the following will show:

Ludwig's angry orders to his servants seldom materialized, most of them remaining mere threats born of momentary nervous irritation. Many such orders were given in very justifiable anger, others were the outcome of passing moods, and were not intended to be taken seriously.

That anybody could stamp up and down, get into a state of blind fury about something, or that the same man should quietly and concentratedly think out some matter without letting his thoughts stray from the subject for one moment, were considered by the servants to be "abnormal" signs.

When the King, either in anger or else simply in fun cried: "That fellow deserves to be locked up, lynched, burnt!" his servants thought that only a madman could say such things. Because their master used to talk to himself, they thought he must necessarily be out of his mind, though Dr. Hubrich, the director of the asylum, was honest enough to admit that sometimes even quite normal people have hallucinations. And when the King once proposed to fly over the Alpsee in an aeroplane his servants were in a great state of excitement. Whatever would they have said to Count Zeppelin?

Gudden believed almost every word of all this disgusting servant's gossip, collecting each little foolishness, each little side-slip in all the forty-one years of Ludwig's life together into one damning piece of evidence to support his diagnosis. If everyone's life were submitted to similar scrutiny we should have to erect countless lunatic asylums for all the otherwise quite harmless people whom we should feel it incumbent upon us to lock up! For instance how many people are there who, similarly to Ludwig II., suffer their whole life long from overwhelming shyness and intense inhibitions when in the presence of others? Must all such beings necessarily be called insane? Or should we not rather find a new expression in psychiatry for this condition?

Ministers responsible for the government had severed themselves almost entirely from personal intercourse with their chief. The circle of the King's own intimate friends became increasingly narrow, while every possible witness for the prosecution was pounced upon, released from his oath of silence on official matters and all his gossip was taken down in writing. Other voices from amongst the people were however intentionally disregarded. People who had spent years of their lives in the neighbourhood of the King were neither called in as witnesses nor even questioned. What was the reason? The leaders of the Catholic party who had repudiated their King, feared evidence in Ludwig's favour. To experienced psychiatrists all these facts will have a serious significance of their own. In any case it is certainly a culpable offence exclusively on the strength of incriminating evidence, without personal observation, without previous conversation with the accused, without warning and with no medical examination, a formality otherwise strictly adhered to, that doctors in official positions should produce a written diagnosis and even defend their action after the King's death!

The following is, for instance, the opinion of *Hofrat* Dr. Hagen: That Ludwig II. in replying to the representations of the Cabinet of the 5th May 1886 should simply have said "it is not the business of the Cabinet to interfere in the matter", is a clear proof of madness! If this be so then countless kings, presidents and directors should have found their way into asylums for similar laconic answers!

Ludwig's prodigious memory—a sure sign of a healthy disposition—was treated by the doctors with scant attention. That his memory towards the end showed little lapses, according to the evidence of the servants, was not taken into account either, though this surely showed that his brain reacted to increasing age like that of any normal man.

As regards this document produced by the doctors, there is one side of the question which was either forgotten or intentionally hushed up, and that is the fact that the Cabinet never made the least effort to rouse the King at the crucial moment to a realization of actual facts. Not only did they omit this obvious duty, but they even encouraged his complete isolation from his people, implanting in him suspicion of the socialists and fears of possible attempts on his life from that quarter. His own ministers placed every possible obstacle in the way of free intercourse between the country and its king, carrying on the formalities of government with little sense of the grave responsibility they were taking upon themselves, Ludwig simply signing what they chose to lay before him.

Finally, when as a logical result of these years of drifting, the King became involved in serious financial difficulties, the minister of finance, far from coming to his king's assistance, publicly repudiated all responsibility, leaving the recluse-king at the mercy of profiteers and on the verge of despair.

Nothing was done in Bavaria to throw light on what had happened. Indeed, after Ludwig's death, those who dared to dissect the events of the past few years, confronting the government with irrefutable facts that would have reinstated the King's honour, were arrested. Of these one need only mention the fate of the out-spoken editor, Memminger.

These are no legends, but bitter truths! And now let us examine the question from the King's own point of view.

Unhindered and untrammelled, Ludwig had ruled in glorious independence, his thoughts intent upon his be-

loved architectural plans, a Gothic castle on the Falkenstein and a castle in enchanting Indian style which he
intended to build on the quiet shores of the Plansee.
All at once he is confronted by a new and superfluous
Commission composed of men who were mainly strangers
to him, who appeared at the castle without previous
appointment. These men inform the ruling King that
he is now under guardianship, that his uncle has taken
over the regency of the country because he, the King,
is out of his mind. Furthermore, he is told that he is
under the orders of these complete strangers and under
the observation, day and night, of keepers whom he
must obey unconditionally, or else he will be put into a
strait-waistcoat !

What was Ludwig's reaction to this flood of information ? Did he fly into a frenzy like a madman ? Did he
hit out in all directions, till he had to be overpowered
and doped ? His reaction was that of any other man
in his senses: he thought out some means of escape.
After one fleeting instant of paralysed surprise at the
inconceivable turn of events, he quickly accomodated
himself to the terrible position into which he had been
put. With a self-control which was truly admirable, he
overcame the bitter humiliation, offering no resistance
whatever to the sudden change from royal freedom to
the ignominy of virtual imprisonment. This was the
reaction of the man whom they declared to be "mad".
He who will maintain that this was typical of the behaviour
of the insane must indeed ask himself why such quiet

collected folks should need asylums, separate cells or strait-waistcoats !

The prisoner was then taken to Berg Castle and introduced on the very first day to all the usual humiliations reserved for the insane. It would have been small wonder had his pride forced him to an ebullition of passionate resistance at having to submit to such indignities. But nothing of the sort took place. From the very first this made such an impression on the brain-specialists that they themselves began to have grave doubts of his insanity.

Bürkel, the last of the court-secretaries with whom Ludwig had come in personal contact, is one of the few honest people who, out of attachment to his master absolutely refused to be led into giving incriminating information of any sort or kind. Similarly, those of Ludwig's servants most intimately acquainted with his habits and who believed in his sanity, refused to give evidence against their master.

One of the oldest government officials, Alexander Schneider, collected three hundred of the King's written orders to the Cabinet of the last three years, orders which Ludwig had always sent by messenger. Not one of these showed the least trace of having been written by one who was out of his mind. Schneider himself had never observed anything of the supposed insanity in all his meetings with the King, least of all at the last audience he had had with Ludwig in May, 1885. He waited to be called to give his evidence before the government——but he waited in vain ! This omission speaks for itself.

All the King's intimate friends, asked whether they had ever noticed signs of derangement, or whether it had remotely occured to them that he might be out of his mind, have answered without reservation in the negative. The most decisive of these was the world-famous actor Josef Kainz. He had spent not only hours but days at a time alone with the King, in Switzerland as well as in Linderhof Castle, having been taken by Ludwig several times through the Blue Grotto. He was one of the last in whom the King confided and had there been anything strange in Ludwig's manner he would certainly have noticed it. As far as his observations went, the King was easily irritated, taking offence at any ill-chosen expression, however unconsciously uttered. This trait greatly enhanced his sense of his royal dignity and ended by forming an impassable barrier between him and the outside world.

The last letter which Ludwig wrote was to his mother, while he was at Linderhof Castle, twelve days before his death and it shows no signs of derangement whatsoever. His mother, though ignorant of the great burden confronting her son of a debt of 21 million marks, had offered him all her jewels which were worth several million. At the time of his tragic departure from Neuschwanstein his thoughts turned gratefully to his absent mother.

Not even the tragic circumstances surrounding his

death could convince the Empress Elisabeth, Ludwig's dearest friend, that he had been out of his mind.

To Count Dürckheim-Monmartin, who had remained faithful to his King when all others had forsaken him, permission was refused to enter the death-chamber to pay his last homage to his master. Dürckheim died, as general in command, in the year 1912 and to his dying day he flatly denied the existence of the least trace of abnormality in the King, for whom he had the deepest devotion.

Bismarck too had believed in Ludwig's sanity until nearly the end, hesitating to accept the theory of insanity. Unfortunately however, the protocol containing the wretched tales told by the castle-servants, instilled doubts into his mind, making him waver. Ludwig had charmed him. He was the only sovereign except the German Emperor, to whom Bismarck in his "Memoirs" dedicated a whole chapter, also publishing some of his letters.

Architects who were actively engaged on the construction of the castles were often surprised at the unfailing accuracy of the King's judgement in architectural questions. They stress the fact that in all the buildings bequeathed by Ludwig to the country there is perfect harmony of detail.

*

Regarding Ludwig's dethronement, the great statesman Bismarck alone, with his admirable insight, was capable of grasping the situation correctly. According to his advice, the Bavarian Cabinet should have put the matter of the King's debts direct before the *Landtag*. Although it was very doubtful whether this particular *Landtag*, which was definitely hostile to the King, would have voted the necessary funds, the settlement of a question of an extremely intimate nature would at least have devolved upon the nation's representatives and not upon the King's near relatives. The Cabinet rejected the Chancellor's wise advice. Bismarck, recognizing the urgent necessity of a regency in Bavaria, insisted on Prussia's neutrality to the whole question, advising other rulers of German federal states, as well as the Austrian Emperor, to refrain from intervention, the matter being one that only concerned Bavaria. Here also the Cabinet refused to be advised and went their own way. This cost their King his life and the ministers themselves have gone down to history with the burden of guilt and the undying hate of the Bavarian people.

Finally the Ministry made themselves a laughing-stock in the eyes of foreign nations by an act which shook not only the sense of patriotism of every good Bavarian, but which surprised the entire world. After declaring Ludwig II. to be out of his mind, taking him prisoner, depriving him of the reins of government and putting him under guardianship———they named as their new king, Ludwig's brother Otto, he whose brain was hopelessly clouded and who was known to be an incurable lunatic ! According to the terms of the Bavarian Constitution, only he could be king who was capable of taking an oath. Prince Otto would never again be capable of undertaking any legal proceeding whatsoever, much less of taking the oath of fidelity to the Constitution in the manner required by law. Ludwig was dethroned on account of a supposed disease, but Otto could become king in spite of suffering in a similar manner. It is hard to see any logic in such a proceeding. One solution of the difficulty would have been to proclaim Luitpold King. Had they done this, it is probable that he would have been far more careful in the choice of his advisers and would have accepted the great responsibility in conjunction with reliable statesmen to assist him. As things were however, as only Prince Regent he was merely at the head of a Cabinet consisting of men who, whether suited to their posts or not, refused to go out of office. From the surplus money accruing to the state owing to the new King being in an asylum and incapable of making use of his allowance, the debts of his dead brother were easily covered. The Ministry remained in office and the Prince Regent remained Prince Regent. They all took the view that at the time of the reorganization they had risked their positions and that now the country owed them a debt of gratitude, for things might have been much worse. That which in June 1886 had been voted impossible, proved in the same month to be workable after all: the Ministry saw their way to balance the budget without going out of their way or putting themselves to any particular trouble.

At the death of Ludwig II., Germany was faced with the inconceivable fact that one of her ruling princes was bankrupt. And to this day there are certain contemporaries who seriously consider Ludwig I. as well as his grandson Ludwig II. to have been mad, maintaining that both of them "threw the money at their disposal out of the window" in foolish building projects, thus running the country into debt in an irresponsible manner.

Has the world ever been enriched by any work of art without the expenditure of great sums of money? Or shall we take as our standard the Egyptian Pharaohs and the Roman Emperors, who made use of slaves, prisoners of war and condemned Christians as forced labour, workers without wage? Was it a case of mad extravagance when a king renounced for years together all great public festivities, using the money which would otherwise have been spent on useless transitory pleasures to produce buildings of permanent value? Is it money "thrown away" when from motives of economy Ludwig used blue colouring-matter instead of costly lapis lazuli from the Ural for the columns of his throne, and instead of porphyry, a clever imitation in brown paint; and that in the place of expensive tapestries he had pictures painted on coarse canvas in imitation? How can one speak of wanton waste when a ruler gives employment to countless artists and workers in his own land, paying them well, giving them the chance to earn a good living, for the beautification of the country, using money for it all from his own privy-purse? Consider what inspiration Ludwig brought to the craftsmen of his country, how he stimulated industry and set money circulating. As late as the year

1882 he opened two great exhibitions, the Arts and Crafts in Nuremberg and the Electrotechnical Exhibition in Munich, finding in the encouragement of work of public utility not only his pleasure but his duty as King. What a wealth of love he poured out upon his land and with what opposition, contradiction and hypocrisy was he rewarded!

But the faint-hearted are not easy to convince. Had they only recognized what significance Wagner would have for future generations, they would neither have refused to remodel the music-school, not rejected his proposal to build a *Festspielhaus* in Munich. That Goethe did not need Duke Karl August of Sax.-Weimar to become Germany's greatest poet beside Schiller, is clear: but Wagner, without his rescuer Ludwig II., would most certainly have been lost to the world. In this connection he once expressed himself in a letter to his patron as follows:

"Without you the *Nibelungen* would never have been written, for had I not been entirely relieved of the struggle for existence I should not have been capable of taking up such an ambitious piece of work again...."

In spite of 77 rehearsals in Vienna, *Tristan und Isolde* was never performed there. Without royal support this opera, after a weak assay in Munich, would have sunk into oblivion. This is common knowledge.

Ludwig I. created a new Munich with his buildings and Ludwig II. has given Upper Bavaria world-wide fame, converting the otherwise poor district around

Füssen and Schwangau into a flourishing self-supporting centre. Beside this, his castles are a source of enormous annual income for Bavaria. Thus the sums of money which were "thrown out of the window" to make of Munich a Wagner-town and to secure Wagner for Bavaria have proved to be the best investment South Germany has ever made. This is an accepted fact.

That the King was cheated right and left is obvious. The history-painter, August von Heckel asked for his picture "Tannhäuser in the Venusberg" which hung in the Blue Grotto at Linderhof 40,000 marks. For a Louis XIV. period writing-table from Paris Ludwig was made to pay 65,000 marks, for an ink-stand with the portraits in enamels of the two French Louis 28,000 marks and for the gold-embroidered curtains for one room alone 65,000 marks. But surely it was the duty of a really able finance minister, one who had the interests of his country at heart to intervene to prevent such unjustifiable over-charging? Ludwig was not able to turn to account the 8 million marks that formed the fortune of his brother Otto who was shut up in Fürstenried, as by Bavarian law no guardian was permitted to make a loan from the property of his ward. Did that justify the ministry in simply laying their hands in their laps and doing nothing? And what is a finance minister for, if not to consider ways and means to realize money and to keep funds moving? Would they not or could they not have thought out some such means of financing the King?

The well-worn reply has too often been heard: "Yes,

but after all, 21 million marks is a fantastic sum !" Remember that in the year 1866, allied to Austria against Prussia Bavaria lost a war that only lasted *one month* and for which she had to pay thirty million gulden. The war was waged against the King's better judgement, fields and forests were destroyed, wounds and death entered thousands of homes. At that time however, there was no question of reproaching the King with this expenditure of funds. On the contrary, the amount was voted at once by Ministry and *Landtag*. Thirty million gulden were required and were immediately forthcoming. Twenty years later the royal household showed a debt of over 20 million marks, neither forest nor field was destroyed, the country indeed beautified and improved, industry stimulated and in all the land no loss by wounds of war. Nor had these debts accumulated in one short month, but in the course of many years. Yet no effort was made to raise the necessary sum. All at once it was said to be impossible to produce money and no one lifted a finger to solve the difficulty. Helplessly they stood by and waited for the inevitable catastrophe. There is no doubt that these are all extremely serious and significant facts which should be taken into account.

*

German historians of that period would have been nearer the truth had they summed up the situation in the following terms:

"Ludwig II. of Bavaria was a born representative of royal ceremony. Though he was mainly instrumental in the founding of the German Empire and though he saved the great composer Richard Wagner for the nation, he suffered grave misunderstanding during his reign. This, after bringing him much personal disappointment, resulted in his leading the life of a recluse. In his solitude he became perhaps one of the greatest romanticists the world has known. Eccentric to a very pronounced degree, he was liable to moods at times almost amounting to hallucinations, which were erroneously mistaken for signs of lunacy. The flourishing state of the country at the time of his death and the fact that he bequeathed his land the most beautiful castles of the world are sufficient proofs that Ludwig II. was one of the most distinguished men of the nineteenth century."

Never before have so many womens' tears been shed over a monarch as over the forty-one-year-old Ludwig. Never before have men weaved so many legends of romance, tragedy and death around a royal figure, as have been written about this king.

A society-lady in Munich was heard to say:

"Strange, that during the King's reign all the world called him mad and now that he is dead no one will hear of his having been out of his mind!"

The Queen-Mother Marie—unhappiest of Bavaria's mothers—out-lived her eldest son by three short years. As she closed her tired eyes for ever in the castle at Hohenschwangau, her last words were:

"God bless Bavaria. God bless Prussia."

Twelve years after Ludwig's tragic end, the Empress Elisabeth fell by the hand of an assassin, in Geneva.

He to whom an early death would have meant deliverance from the tortures of life—King Otto—suffered 68 years the bondage of disease.

Can flesh be heir to greater tragedies than these? This is the end of the story, nor can history reveal more. Only truth lives on down the ages. The truth about the royal recluse shall live on, imperishable as are the memorials he has bequeathed us, his incomparable works!

Sources of information.

Gottfried von Böhm: Ludwig II., König von Bayern, Sein Leben und seine Zeit.
Berlin 1924, Engelmann.

Anton Memminger. Der Bayernkönig Ludwig II., Würzburg.

Clara Tschudi: König Ludwig II. von Bayern. Reclam, Leipzig.

Hans Steinberger: Der Romantiker Ludwig II. auf dem Königsthron. Kaufbeuern, Vereinigte Kunstanstalten.

Fritz Linde: Ich, der König, der Untergang Ludwigs II. Kummers Verlag, Leipzig.

Walter Rummel: König und Kabinettsschef. München 1919.

Carl Franz Müller: Die letzten Tage König Ludwigs II. Berlin 1888, Fischer.

Edir Grein: Tagebuchaufzeichnungen von Ludwig II., König von Bayern. 1925.

Richard Wagner: Mein Leben. Volksausgabe. München 1911.

Sebastian Röckl: Ludwig II. und Richard Wagner. 2 Bände. München 1913 und 1920.

Weißheimer: ,,Erlebnisse." Stuttgart 1898.

Bismarck: Gedanken und Erinnerungen.

Rudolf Helmers: Dienstbericht an die Schwangauer Feuerwehr.

Ferdinand Boppeler: Eidliches Protokoll des Gendarmeriewachtmeisters von Hohenschwangau.

Mang Anton Niggl: Aufzeichnungen (im Besitz der Schwangauer Feuerwehr).

Carl v. Washington: ,,Die letzten Tage des Königs Ludwig II. von Bayern."
Aufzeichnungen eines Augenzeugen (von seiner Witwe im Jahre 1932 der Öffentlichkeit übergeben).

Notice: To rigorously exlude all possibility of historical misrepresentation, incontestable facts, actions and conversations have, in part, been taken verbatim from the above mentioned works in all points concerning actual history, as distinguished from those that constitute the author's own poetic embellishment.

Lightning Source UK Ltd.
Milton Keynes UK
UKHW022322060223
416579UK00001B/317